**HIGHBURY
ENTERTAINMENT**
A HIGHBURY HOUSE COMMUNICATIONS PLC COMPANY

**Highbury Entertainment Ltd, Paragon House,
St Peters Road, Bournemouth, Dorset. BH1 2JS**

Tel: +44 (0)1202 299900
Fax: +44 (0)1202 299955
Email: books@paragon.co.uk
www.paragon.co.uk

Written by:..................... ANDY HARTUP
Designed by..................... ANDREW DOWNES
Sub Editor:..................... KAREN RUTHEFORD
Printed & bound in the UK by: .... MACKAYS OF CHATHAM, BADGER ROAD,
                                   LORDSWOOD, CHATHAM, KENT, ME5 8TD

HALO
EVOLVED

The true story of Bungie's
legendary Xbox game

THE HISTORY OF HALO

There isn't an Xbox owner alive that hasn't heard of Bungie, the legendary creator of the *Halo* series, but it wasn't always that way. As with every success story, there is a beginning, a middle, but no real end to speak of. After all, everyone knows that the developer is busy beavering away on its next project, and that this game – no matter what it turns out to be – will mark yet another massive stage in the evolution of gaming as a whole. Yes, it's probably going to be *Halo 3*. You know it. We know it. Microsoft knows it: but no official confirmation will exist until the world's largest Xbox developer is good and ready to show it off.

So, where did Bungie actually start? Well, the real answer to this question is Chicago, USA. Bungie was started in 1991 by a chap named Alex Seropian, who eagle-eyed readers will know has gone on to found another studio known as Wideload Games, which is working on a title called *Stubbs The Zombie: Rebel Without a Pulse*. Seropian was an ambitious chap who needed a team to work on his self-planned title called *Operation: Desert Storm*. He formed an alliance with classmate Jason Jones, who had also been working on a new Mac project named *Minotaur*. Together, the two of them produced both games for market on a real shoestring budget, with the small reward being that their first game *Operation: Desert Storm* sold a miniscule 2,500 copies. However, the real success from the early days was *Minotaur*…

The game *Minotaur: The Labyrinths of Crete* developed an incredibly select hardcore following because it made use of AppleTalk and Modems, something that was virtually unheard of in 1992. Again the game shifted 2,500 units, but Jones and Seropian had started to build up a small, but elite, fan following. The next game was essentially *Minotaur* from a first-person perspective and was known as *Pathways Into Darkness*. It was one of the most visually striking games of the time and it earned the team (which had now acquired graphics coder Colin Brent) all sorts of accolades including an entry into MacWorld's Hall Of Fame and several top 100 game lists. This was when the cash started to flow into Bungie, allowing the team to get more creative with their projects, and more importantly turn themselves into a real development company.

After a rather shaky start, Bungie finally decided to start work on a sequel to *Pathways Into Darkness*, but this time around, it would be set in a spaceship and would have aliens instead of ancient monsters. It would have friendly AI and gorgeous 3D visuals, along with some truly intense first-person gameplay. It would be the greatest Mac game of all time. It would be *Marathon*.

Released in 1994, *Marathon* won awards, bettered all the PC games of the time, such as *Doom* and *Descent*, and more importantly, it made Bungie the premiere Mac developer in the world almost overnight. The cash rolled in and work started immediately on a much-demanded sequel. The next game, *Marathon 2: Durandal* was even more advanced than the original and it introduced all sorts of new and exciting multiplayer modes. Essentially, *Durandal* gave birth to some of the most popular *Halo* game modes of today, including King Of The Hill, a very familiar mode called Kill The Man With The Ball, and Campaign Co-Operative play. The year was 1995 and Bungie had become a force to be reckoned with, as its growth increased by 500%.

The *Marathon* team then went to work on a new project that became *Myth*, one of the most critically acclaimed Real Time Strategy titles ever made. It shipped simultaneously on Mac and PC and to date, the title has sold around 350,000 units. We say to date, because fans are still playing it just under 10 years on – *Myth* spawned a host of sequels and became one of the most played online titles of the time. During this period several key members of the current Bungie staff climbed on board, including sound guru Marty O'Donnell, who had just completed work on 1996's *Riven*.

This isn't to say everything was sweet and rosy. Bungie's first colossal title had a patchy past that nearly ended the party prematurely. Just before even a single boxed copy of then original *Myth* was due to hit the stores, someone found a bug. No big deal right? Well, what if we were to tell you that this bug deleted the entire computer's Hard Drive in one go? Bungie employees were forced to march down to the factory, open up the ready-to-roll boxes of the game, and swap each one for versions that didn't contain the problem: expensive, and a big setback for the developer. However, undeterred the team set to work on its next title.

A group of employees moved out of Chicago and headed west to form an arm of the company imaginatively titled Bungie West, the offices for which were based in San Jose, California. This team started work on *Oni*, the developer's first console title, which was snapped up by Take 2 and released on the PS2 in 1999. Take 2 was so impressed that it bought a 20% stake in the developer and this injected them with that all-important cash as well as worldwide developer status.

What was to come next took the world by storm, and firmly established Bungie as a household name for the digital generation. And this all took place at the Macworld Show in 1999, a trade event that would change the world of games forever as the first threads of what was to become *Halo* came together.

HALO
THE
EARLY
YEARS

Halo wasn't always an Xbox title. It started life as a little-known Mac game that was first shown at the Macworld Show in 1999. Initially it was a Real Time Strategy title, and Bungie claims that it still has a code that allows players to fight with waves of human soldiers and vehicles – a little like *Myth* in space. However, this was to change when in 2000, Microsoft saw the *Halo* project and immediately stepped in to buy the game, Bungie, and all the employees for a considerable bundle of cash. This meant that Microsoft had its killer IP for the launch of the still unborn Xbox, and Bungie was set for the future.

At the time, PC and Mac owners were decidedly unhappy about the move, and here is a selection of letters written to Bungie, which were then subsequently answered by their Webmaster:

"I have been a fan of Bungie ever since *Marathon* a few years back. I have also been a Microsoft hater ever since their beginning, swallowing up companies like it was going out of style. I have many reasons to hate this up-and-coming Xbox and now you come along and join Microsoft. How could you do this? This email may not concern this site, but it concerns your entire company. I have decided to dislike you and so have many of my friends. I hope you lose a lot of business because of this self-inflicted punishment you have just given yourself."

"Hello Mr Webmaster. Being fans of all Bungie games, we were aghast at the Microsoft acquisition of Bungie Software. We are creating a website dedicated to freeing Bungie, because we fear you have been brainwashed, and causing the downfall of Microsoft through comical editorials."

"Microsoft = Borg, and Bungie has been assimilated. Unfortunately, contrary to what you believe, after *Halo*, you will be dissipated. Bad move."

"To put it bluntly, you have just signed the end to Bungie. I have been a fan of Bungie for years – that just ended. I am totally disgusted that you have sold out the Mac community for that low-life bastard Bill Gates. I have every game you have ever released. I was going to buy *Oni* – not any more. I am not the only Mac user who feels that way; you can forget about supporting the Macintosh platform anymore, you've had it. I hope you have the sense not to go through with this."

"Okay, maybe I'm having a nightmare. Am I going crazy or has one of the best game companies reached an ultimate low? Did I read the article correctly? Are you actually selling out to Microsoft? I can't believe such an amazing company could do this. I don't care if the consequences are good or bad; I mean come on! It's fucking MICROSOFT for God's sake. Sorry to rant at you, but I have never actually been pissed off at a company until this."

This represents a selection from what probably amounted to hundreds of irritated Bungie fans. They were an angry mob because at the time it was assumed that there would be no PC or Mac versions of *Halo*. However, this was 2000, and many quite rightly assumed that because Microsoft owned Bungie, this meant that *Halo* was exclusive to Xbox. *Oni* honoured its agreement with Take 2 and released in 2001, and the whole Bungie team moved up to Redmond, Seattle where the Microsoft Campus was situated. Hilariously, Bungie quotes on its website that one of its coders famously said of *Halo*, "We never got it running on PS2 anyway". It was at this point that one of the founder members, Alex Seropian, decided to leave Bungie for pastures new and eventually set up Wideload Studios. The leaving party for Seropian (and the move from Chicago) was held in the original Bungie office-apartment, after the company offered the lucky current tenant $1000 to host the event at the nostalgic site.

Meanwhile work continued on *Halo*, and Bungie was starting to feel the pressure that came with launching its title on a completely new platform in time for that console's launch. *Halo*, after an initial underwhelming showing at that year's E3 was in fact becoming the killer-app for the original Xbox, and Microsoft was relying upon the boys based in Seattle to deliver the goods. On 15 November 2001 the game launched to an expectant American audience, and once again, after a shaky start for the console itself, the sales started to roll in as people discovered that, not only did *Halo* look the business, but it also had fantastic gameplay balance and tip-top multiplayer. It was to be the start of a legend, and very soon the world started demanding to know when Bungie would be delivering the sequel.

HALO HITS THE SHELVES

X360's sister magazine *XBM* got hold of a copy of *Halo* when the console launched in the UK, and the review was an emphatic tribute to what the game offered the new console:

"Imagine perfection. Just consider for one moment what it would be like to find a game in any genre that you would be happy to play until the cows came home, got bored and strolled off into the fields again. Well in the world of first-person shooters the only name you need to know is *Halo*.

It's actually quite worrying when you think about it. Because from the moment you start playing this game you realise that no matter what happens after this, all first-person shooters that follow are going to be compared to this. To have a game this amazingly good on day one brings tears of joy to our eyes. Everything in *Halo* is going to make you praise the day you were born – needless to say when beginning to review a game like this it's difficult to know where to begin!

The first thing you'll notice about this life-changing masterpiece is just how much it feels like a film. The story of a marine on an alien world has been done countless times before, but the twists in the plot are as engaging as any Hollywood blockbuster – better in some cases! We're not going to spoil the story for you here but believe us when we say you're not going to be skipping any of the cut-scenes – all of which are produced in real-time on the Xbox!

One very memorable moment comes when you enter a room to find blood all over the walls from the bodies strewn across the floor – and you just know they didn't die a peaceful death! A cut-scene follows as your marine picks up a discarded helmet and watches back the grainy video feed prior to the group's death. The atmosphere created is intense and sends a chill down your spine that you could cool a six-pack with."

This was the rebirth of the first-person shooter on console, and the critics had started to pick up on it with absolute relish. It was at this point that Bungie decided to announce that it hadn't forgotten about its faithful following, and was preparing versions of the mighty *Halo* for both PC and favoured platform Mac. The response on Bungie.net was truly phenomenal, and it certainly seemed like the fans had forgiven Bungie for its dealings with the 'evil' Microsoft:

"I just wanted to thank all the people at Bungie who brought us *Halo*. For the past few years I have had an addiction to *Halo* that some would call unhealthy, but I don't listen to them. *Halo* was the reason I bought my Xbox, and the reason why my grades have been steadily dropping lately. I spent more time playing Halo last year than I did studying for school, doing homework, doing work around the house, and eating combined. I have missed all three meals before because I would rather play Halo than get my lazy ass over to the fridge. Yesterday I called my boss and told him I wouldn't

be able to go to work that day because I was too sick. When really I just wanted to get a good Blood Gulch CTF session in with my homies. *Halo* has turned me into a mess and I wouldn't change it for the world."

Indeed, Halo Lan parties had become one of the most popular pastimes for early Xbox adopters, and before the advent of Live a year after the console's initial release, the finest way to enjoy multiplayer action was to lug your Xbox round to a friend's house for some System Linked *Halo*. Many claim that the multiplayer of the original was easily the best part of the game, but for most, the hassle that was involved in actually setting up these games was far greater than the quick thrill that the multiplayer offered. Xbox gamers needed some sort of global broadband network in order to experience *Halo* as it was meant to be played. The PC and Mac versions would be a good start, but Xbox Live would be the ideal solution to this problem.

BEYOND THE XBOX

Whereas many keen gamers had waited patiently for *Halo* to release on the PC and Mac, when it did actually arrive, the response was a mixed bag from the critics. A few Microsoft haters lurked in the depths of the internet, and they slammed the game for a supposedly poor frame rate and inferior control options. This probably stung Bungie a little, especially as the home computer versions were a pet-project for them, rather than being a requirement from new owners Microsoft. Perhaps the haters will be less inclined to bring their prejudices to the table when demanding that Bungie release *Halo 2* for the Mac and PC.

The fans, on the other hand, were elated, and the only people who really missing out on the *Halo* action were the chumps that stuck with the PS2 and GameCube without venturing beyond their platforms of choice. Try as they might though, none could persuade Bungie to break their exclusivity deal with Microsoft and bring out sub-standard versions of the game for GameCube and PS2:

"I am wondering why don't you make *Halo* and *Halo 2*
for PlayStation and PlayStation2?
I really like the game and everything, but for people with PlayStation2s and ones, don't you think it's a little unfair?"

"Well here I am, you said you wanted to talk to me about GameCube buying Bungie and I was thinking that this might be a good idea but now I am not sure. I mean I really do love GameCube but I think that it could buy Bungie, it's just I don't know how you will feel about being bought.

   Please email me fast, I only have one day to get back to GameCube to tell them your reply."

   In fact, to this day, PS2 and GameCube magazines still receive letters from less-informed gamers demanding to know why *Halo* will never be appearing on their respective consoles, and this mail usually elicits the same sort of sarcastic response as has been given by Bungie's Webmaster time and time again on the subject. It really is a foregone conclusion that no *Halo* game will ever appear on any other console than that which carries the Xbox brand – end of story.

   However, one question that did produce a few positive responses from Bungie's Webmaster concerned a follow-up to the original game. After their initial taste of this brilliant new franchise, loyal Xbox owners were already demanding to know what the developer was planning next. This was summed up in a letter to Bungie.net that simply said:

   "I am a big fan of *Halo*....
   Do you know if you will make a second game or not?"

   The answer was obviously "Yes", and at E3 2003 – a mere two years on from the original title's release – fans were given a taste of what was to come. Sure there had been an initial teaser video along with a handful of screens, but this time the game was in motion and it looked deliciously good…

HALO 2
THE
WAIT

Ever since *Halo 2* was announced, it seemed like the whole world was completely gripped by *Halo* fever. Every scrap of information surrounding the game was always pounced upon with relish, and the rumours started to spread like wildfire from the start. Quite simply, the release was always going to be the most significant event in Xbox, and as it turns out, entertainment history. However, the wait was a long one, and the game was delayed a whole year from its initial release date, before finally hitting the shelves in November 2004.

When the first few images of the game started to roll in, the world went *Halo 2* crazy, but the real surprises were waiting for fans at E3 2003, when the Bungie bandwagon really began to pick up speed. Here is our first real preview of the game, as it appeared in *XBM* at the time:

"Picture the scene. A camera swoops down through the Earth's atmosphere and then over Africa, closing in on the southeast of the continent. We hover for a moment over a sprawling megalopolis, quite unlike any African city of this century. This is obviously the future. A caption comes up informing us that this is indeed New Mombasa, a city of steel and glass, a technological utopia and a jewel in the crown of human achievement… and it is currently under heavy attack from alien forces!

A Pelican drop ship swoops down above us and the scene cuts to the

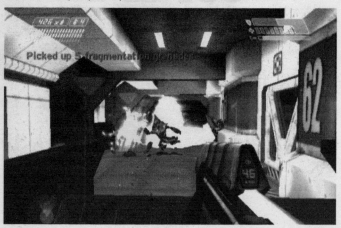

Master Chief staring out at the city under siege. The radio crackles into life and the drop ship's crew are informed that the area is too hot for a landing. They land anyway…

We find ourselves behind the human frontline and things look bad. Soldiers lie around, some wounded and being attended by medics, some not so lucky. The surrounding buildings lie in ruins and plasma blasts make the ground tremble with their impacts. It's clear that the Covenant forces are closing in quickly on human positions and something is going to be have to done quickly if they're not to be overrun. Cue the Master Chief…

So the scene is set for Bungie's E3 demo of *Halo 2*, a graphical and technical exploration and mouthwatering taster of what they have in store for the finished game, a statement of intent by the best development team working on Xbox. Boy, is it special.

The first thing revealed is the extent of your immersion in a computer-generated world. It's like some kind of interactive cut-scene being played out – or you're viewing a movie from the first-person – the aforementioned injured soldiers are interacting with medics, the uninjured Marines defend positions from attacks (and get blown up) and all the while you get this feeling of belonging in this world. There's radio chatter, there's shouting and screaming, explosions, gunfire; it's like you've just walked into a nightmare.

The second thing we find out is the role that Cortana now plays. Your

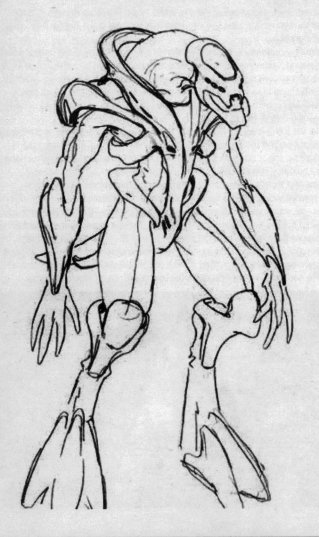

female AI companion from the first game is now more tactical advisor than clinger on – she more than earns her keep as she quickly informs you where the next threat is coming from and how you might deal with it. She also talks to the ground troops, advising them on tactics and gleaning info. It all helps in making the *Halo 2* game world all the more believable.

And you need her help, because the next thing that becomes apparent is that this is no skirmish – *Halo 2* is a full-on war. The number of enemies coming at you – and the amount of friendlies fighting alongside you – is quite incredible. Teams of Grunts and Elites assaulting human positions – sometimes repelled, sometimes successful, but always working together in a believable way; and whether or not it's just the ambience, it all seems coordinated, it all seems very real…

More importantly, though, Master Chief is using a new weapon – he's got a new rifle – it's a combination of the assault rifle and the pistol from the first game. It has a zoom function like the pistol but fires more rapidly – the Master Chief needs that extra speed, as Grunts and Jackals are everywhere. Fortunately there's a mounted gun position nearby. The Chief grabs the gun and the camera pulls back to third-person revealing more of the action around him – a few blasts on the cannon and the immediate enemy threat is over… for a moment.

Then the Chief is given his next weapon, two – yeah, count them – two machine pistols. The pistols are fired by using the left and right analogue triggers – they can be fired individually or as one. The Chief opts for the 'as one' option – after all, it would be rude not to. He runs down into the melee…Then there's the rush of combat – the Chief dashes through the ruins, exterminating Grunts, sometimes alone, sometimes with the aid of Marines working in groups. Next thing you know, there's a group of Warthogs up front. The Chief jumps into the back of one, electing to take the gun instead of the wheel… and we're treated to the sight of tearing around city blocks at high speed taking out Covenant ships, troops, parked cars… and all with a brand new rocket launcher.

And then, as if from nowhere, a Brute lands on the 'hog, knocks out the driver and causes the jeep to crash! What? Where did that one come from? The Chief is quick to sort the situation out – a quick hit of the new combo melee move is enough to sort out the Brute…

But then a new attack! Ghosts scream toward the Chief but he stands his ground, waiting… and then he jumps, landing squarely on the front of the Ghost, kicking out its driver and clambers into the seat. Anything you can do,

I can do better, eh? And we're into a cut-scene – a chase sequence – and then we're left on a cliffhanger, with the Chief surrounded by light sword-wielding Elites, double machine pistols in hands…

It was just a glimpse of what *Halo 2* will offer, only intended to show some of the features and new moves that have already been implemented. But it won't stop there – Bungie is bound to keep some stuff over for a big surprise. The story? The extent of the Covenant invasion? Exactly what has happened to Guilty Spark and his battle with the Flood? Where are the rest of the Halos? All these questions and more will be answered when the game is released next year. Hell, we don't even know if this level will make it into the final game… What we do know, is that it shows just what every Xbox owner wanted to know: that *Halo 2* will be better than the original. And considering that has yet to be bettered by any game on Xbox, that is quite some feat. Here's to Bungie… If the final game is going to be better than this, then take as long as you like, boys."

The world was stunned by the possibilities of Dual-Wielding, vehicle boarding and the thought of fighting the Covenant on home turf. Throughout the next year and a half, speculation was rife about what the single-player campaign would offer. What were those hairy creatures driving the Ghosts? What was the role of the Prophet? Why had the Covenant come to Earth? All these questions and more were whirling around inside fans'

brains for a whole year, until the next step was proudly announced at E3 2004. All thoughts of the single player were virtually abandoned as Bungie revealed its plans for the new Live enabled multiplayer side of things, as witnessed by *XBM*…

" 'Oh my god. Oh my god. Oh my goaaaaaaad!' These are not the screams of an American witnessing an act of despicable terrorism, nor is it the sound of Jordan in the company of the England footy captain. Oh no, this is the noise of every person who witnessed the playable unveiling of Bungie's latest offering at this year's E3 games show. More shocking than 9/11 and better than celebrity sex, ladies and gentlemen *XBM* would like to present *Halo 2*.

The game has such a history; it's difficult to know where to begin. Anyone who saw last year's rolling demo of this historic title will know that the Master Chief's comeback is an epic affair, and Microsoft is really banking on this baby to shift the big black boxes we all know and love this Christmas. Judging by what we've seen here, Santa will be in need of some serious deep muscle massaging after delivering sacks packed to the brim with *Halo 2* Xbox bundles to all the kiddies around the world on Xmas eve. It's also going to be a bugger for the dustmen come New Year – what the hell will they do with all those wasted PS2s?

Okay, sales speculation aside, the first and most obvious impact *Halo 2* had on the crowds was its graphical flare and sheer special impact. Fans of

all things *Halo* and Bungie will have been devouring the weekly updates like hungry pack animals, so many will be aware that the scale is huge. *Halo 2* is indeed massive, and more to the point, it's so damn detailed. Trees sway in the breeze, vehicles leave imprints in the road or gravel, bullet holes and puckering can be seen in the war-torn streets and the Master Chief has his fair share of battle scars. One new element is the addition of scenery interaction, which adds an extra dimension of reality to the game.

Pass-out moment number two has to be the new weapon system, which allows the Chief to wield two different weapons at once. Blast a Jackal's shield with an energy pistol, then finish him off with a human one. The possibilities are massive for this system! Then there's the Chief's new rifle; the one seen in last year's demo, that works like a rifle with a sniper scope attached; perfect for picking off enemies in the enormous environments. What are these massive levels of which we speak? Well, Bungie has finally confirmed the locations in which the game takes place. The action starts off on Earth, ravaged by a bloody war with the Covenants, but later on the Chief will find himself on… wait for it… another Halo ring. That's right, the plot most definitely thickens when MC obtains the information regarding another Halo, and the possible uses to which the Covenant will put it.

And then there's the multiplayer. Xbox Live support was always going to be a given considering the high-profile nature of this game, but the extent of this wasn't really known before E3. Multiplayer maps are indeed huge, allowing the player to use height as well as width to wage war on their opponents. Screens show a number of these levels in use, and from these you should be able to gain some sense of the sheer scale. *Halo* was massive, but *Halo 2* is in a different league. The new mode, Assault, is a bomb-style option that pits the four teams (oh, yes) against each other for control of a map. Vehicles are available in multiplayer, much like they were in the first game, but this time several modifications have been employed. Examples of this are the Banshees and Ghosts, which can now be pushed to mind-boggling speeds in order to cover ground quicker in the more open levels.

There's so much to say about *Halo 2*, so expect plenty more information to seep out in the coming months. One thing that is expected is the release date, which many are still mooting as early September."

The world was certainly ready for some serious *Halo 2* love, and Microsoft finally confirmed that the date of release was to be 9 November in the US (surprisingly in the form of a tattoo on the arm of Corporate Vice President of Worldwide Marketing, Peter Moore), and 11 November in the UK. Fans would be playing the sequel to their favourite game within the year, and the wait was finally drawing to a close. However, for some, the game couldn't come soon enough and *Halo 2* ran into the ugly world of piracy…

HALO 2 – THE RELEASE

So, it was October 2004, and *Halo 2* was knocking on Xbox's door demanding to be let in. The world was bracing itself for the influx of *Halo*-hungry shoppers, all demanding their copies of the Limited Edition tin that would be made available for early adopters, when a minor disaster occurred – the game had leaked onto the internet.

The edition that first appeared was in French, strongly suggesting that a light-fingered Gallic Microsoft employee had snatched a copy from the distribution warehouse and uploaded it onto the net. However, shortly after this version appeared, English language copies also started to rear their ugly heads on piracy sites, forcing Microsoft to issue stern warnings for those who sought to distribute illegal copies of *Halo 2*. The lawyers had been informed, and they were hungry for blood. Microsoft was not about to let a few angry geeks spoil their party.

One source that did manage to get its hands on a legal version of the game, before its UK release, was *XBM*, and this was their reaction to the finished

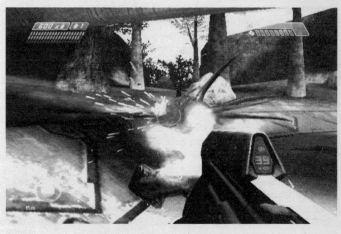

product, which naturally received a perfect 10/10 in the magazine:

"There are no secrets in this review. No plot twists, no spoilers, not even hints at what the player can expect from the most anticipated release in the history of home entertainment. Sure, we could blab about the inner workings of the game – it's out now, and we don't doubt that hundreds of forum users will be desperately trying to broadcast every last detail in an attempt to show how great they are for finishing *Halo 2* quicker than their virtual buddies.

Halo 2 is more than a game. It's a brilliant, infinitely honed experience that sucks its audience in with shiny visuals, wows them with the slickest gameplay created, and keeps them on the edge of the seat with some of the most innovative and intelligent features available. So, barricade your door, rip the internet connection from its socket, switch off the mobile phone, and don't stop playing the game until the bitter end.

The single-player element of Halo 2 has been one of the most closely guarded secrets around, and although much has been made of the game's fine multiplayer, the scraps of information surrounding Master Chief's latest campaign have been few and far between. It's generally known that Earth comes under attack from a Covenant force, and that the Chief is back in time to lend a helping hand and a size-fourteen boot to kick some serious alien ass (or whatever they have). Right from the word 'go' it's obvious that *Halo 2* has evolved with the capabilities of the Xbox, as the opening cut-scenes are a vast improvement on those from the original game, lending a distinctly movie-like quality to the series. Bungie is well aware that it has been toiling away on the sequel to a game that has spawned millions of fans, and the storyline reflects this from the outset. Whereas this will enthral anyone who has played the original, newcomers may feel a little disorientated at the start of proceedings. However, as the story progresses, the back-history is slowly filtered through, bringing fresh *Halo* converts quickly up to speed with the universe that Bungie built. In fact, *Halo 2* really does reveal the scope and depth of Master Chief's world in a way that the first game only hinted at. The plot twists, surprises and all manner of cheeky little gameplay tweaks flow thick and fast, giving the whole experience a constantly fresh feeling that is second to none in the world of gaming.

Halo 2 feels like a Hollywood blockbuster, and although that term is bandied about to describe every two-bit action game on console, it almost feels as if the expression has found its one true home. Some events are scripted, but these are few and far between, leaving the rest of the game's enormous

levels as a violent playground for Master Chief and his weapons of choice. There are, as is to be expected, plenty of new weapons to experience, all of which feel extremely natural within the confines of the gameplay engine. After a couple of kills, chances are you'll wonder how you ever lived without the Battle Rifle or the Covenant Energy sword. Dual wielding is incredibly simple, yet it is an absolutely essential addition to the *Halo* style of play that fits in neatly with all the other tweaks and modifications. Much has been made of the fact that the new pistol, now known as the Magnum, has no zoom – but this is adequately compensated for by the Battle Rifle, which is a far better medium ranged zoom weapon than the old pistol. Another concern was that Master Chief no longer has a health bar. Indeed, once the energy shield has run out, you'd better dive for cover, but this is balanced out by the fact that recharge happens much quicker, and the fact that the game has dual wielding. By shifting the focus from worrying about health, to the more basic attitude of 'killing him, before he kills me' Bungie has given the *Halo* series a new pace that players of the original could only dream of.

This, coupled with the game's new level design, makes for an experience that is exactly what is to be expected from *Halo 2*. Much like the relationship between *Burnout 2* and *3*, the new game has somehow eclipsed its hugely popular forerunner by some distance. One of the complaints that casual *Halo* players had of the original was that some of the levels were too long and

repetitive, and when the backtracking started, many gave up on the whole thing. *Halo 2*'s levels are masterfully crafted, and even though a tiny amount of repetition has found its way back into the game, the action never feels like a chore while you're struggling back through familiar territory. This could be due to the fact that vehicles are offered up as a potentially larger part of the game; maybe it's the way that the levels are more detailed; or perhaps it's because the AI has been given a massive overhaul, leaving the player in no doubt that they're in the centre of something truly epic. Either way, it's a safe bet that none of the levels will be bemoaned in the same way that The Library and The Silent Cartographer were in *Halo*'s original outing.

The new AI, both enemy and friendly, is a real reflection of the leap that the series has taken, and chances are you'll be far too busy dealing with them to be worried about taking in the admittedly breathtaking scenery. Covenant Elites have been given a new lease of life in the game, and now they'll behave exactly as you'd expect them to, which includes ducking behind cover, climbing over obstacles to attack your position and hijacking the vehicles you're riding in. Balancing this, friendly characters have been upgraded too and will find appropriate cover, shout out directions about where they think the enemy are hiding, and use weapons to suit their situation. According to Bungie there are thousands of combat phrases in the game, and although we didn't count them, having played the game for several days and only heard a

couple of comments twice, we'd be inclined to believe this boast. The Marines and the much-loved Sergeant Johnson keep the banter levels high throughout the game adding comic relief and an extra level of immersion that few other games have even touched upon.

If there is one key phrase that sums up the *Halo 2* experience then it would have to be engaging. The swanky visuals, the gorgeous sound score that helps stir the senses of excitement and awe in equal measures, and the carefully considered plot, all blend together to allow the player a chance to really engage with the game. This is an amazing feat, as even some of the world's most popular blockbusters struggle to maintain audience attention for three hours of cinema time. Even without multiplayer, *Halo 2* is much more substantial than the previous game, with later levels sprawling into epic distances that require a serious chunk of time to simply walk all the way through. The addition of Live support and the continued support of a co-operative mode expands the game's play time to a state that is almost as epic as the game itself, and it's a safe bet that millions will still be playing this one for years and years to come. Co-op is just as slick as it was, despite the fact that there are probably double the number of enemies on screen at any given time, making it an aspect of the game that begs to be experienced – especially if you don't happen to own Xbox Live. Everyone with online gaming capabilities are in for double the treat, as it could be argued that

Halo 2 multiplayer is not only leagues ahead of any other broadband enabled game, but it may even leave the single-player experience in the shadows. The options for online play are far more varied than even Ubisoft's Clancy titles, and the interface and lobby systems represent everything that Xbox Live is truly capable of.

Halo 2 is massive. Most will buy it purely because it's the sequel to the most played Xbox title ever. Others will pick up a copy because their mates have told them to, and a vast number will even buy an Xbox to be part of it all. However, unlike Driv3r, which sold regardless of its dearth of quality, Microsoft's game deserves all the sales it can manage, because the end result is something that is truly stunning. *Halo 2* is a wonderful testament, not only to the power and potential of the Xbox, but also to the capability of videogames to amaze, entertain, and capture the imagination of their players. To employ yet another clichéd phrase: the best things come to those who wait. We have waited, and Bungie has certainly delivered the best.

THE AFTERMATH

Once the dust had settled from the game's launch, which included numerous midnight openings of games stores, a pre-order frenzy like none that has ever gone before, and one wild party in Times Square and later on at London

Bridge, the stats started to roll in. Naturally, *Halo 2* had made it to the top of the UK charts, beating off competition from heavyweights such as *Need for Speed Underground 2* and *Grand Theft Auto San Andreas*. This was put into perspective through the announcement that the game was the most significant event in entertainment history, as it had made $125 million in the first day of sale. That record easily beats any film, book, or other game to this date, and even the release of the latest *Harry Potter* novel failed to match the achievement of *Halo 2*, with Rowling's effort only managing to net $100 million on the first weekend of sale (not that the Brit novelist will be complaining too much!).

The franchise continues to sell extremely well, and to this day *Halo 2* remains in the top 20 chart for the Xbox in both the UK and the US. All in all, 13 million copies of the *Halo* series have been sold, and the split is now pretty even between the original and the sequel. Many sources quote an exact 50:50 ratio, with the original and the second game clocking up 6.5 million units each. However, as the Xbox user-base continues to grow, expect the second game to outpace its forerunner in terms of copies shifted. Regardless of how it is split, the sales mean that both Bungie and Microsoft's futures in the console market are assured.

HALO 2 FROM THE INSIDE

As is to be expected, the game started to spill its secrets to an eagerly awaiting world, and it was not long before people had played the single-player aspect of the game to death. Anyone wondering about the contents of the game should check out this brief guide to the world of *Halo 2*:

VEHICLES

All the vehicles in the game can now be destroyed, including the Warthog. It's also possible to steal vehicles (and have them stolen from you) by holding down the X button. Here's how best to use each of the rides in the game:

WARTHOG

The Warthog comes in two varieties – regular and gauss – with the latter firing explosive shells. Warthogs need at least two people to use effectively, as it's not possible to drive and shoot at the same time. However, having a separate gunner allows the vehicle to move in one direction while shooting in another. It's a quick and versatile vehicle that's best used by darting in and out with hit-and-run tactics. Use the Warthog's speed and handling to get behind enemy vehicles, as most of them can only fire forwards.

GHOST

This is a single-seater Covenant craft. It's manoeuvrable and carries an upgraded version of the Plasma Rifle that doesn't suffer from overheating. It's also possible to speed up the Ghost by holding L, but this deactivates your weapons and affects the vehicle's handling.

However, you'll find that Ghosts don't tend to last particularly long, as their armour leaves something to be desired. Therefore it's best to ditch your Ghost after it's taken a few hits, or you could find yourself very dead, very quickly. Fight by keeping a good distance from your enemies and strafe in order to avoid their shots. If you do this, you should be able to take down vehicles like Wraiths easily.

SPECTRE

This new addition is the Covenant's version of the Warthog. As such, it's not possible to drive a Spectre and shoot at the same time. The Spectre carries a powerful energy weapon that's harder to aim than the Warthog's turret. Like Ghosts, Spectres are able to strafe and it's possible to increase their speed by holding the L button, at the cost of handling. Use Spectres in a similar way to Warthogs when fighting other vehicles: try to get alongside or behind them, so they can't hit you with their weapons.

SCORPION TANK

The Scorpion Tank is simply godlike in single player, but its slow speed makes it easy to hijack. It has a powerful cannon, capable of destroying Ghosts in a single hit. This doesn't fire all that often, but is backed up by a machine gun with an endless supply of ammo. This vehicle is well armoured and a match for anything you care to throw at it. However, it's best to keep your distance from Wraiths, as the Scorpion's speed means it won't be able to dodge their attacks if you get too close.

WRAITH

The Wraith is incredibly powerful, but is somewhat harder to use than the Scorpion Tank. This is because the Wraith fires a slow, arcing projectile, while the Scorpion shoots its cannon directly and instantly. This can sometimes work to your advantage though, as the Wraith can shoot over obstacles and hit targets without them firing back. This makes it handy for shelling cliff tops from underneath, where other vehicles would only be able to hit enemies standing near the edge. Like the other Covenant vehicles, the Wraith can access a speed boost by holding L. This is extremely useful for knocking Ghosts out of the way, as you won't be able to hit them if they're right next to you.

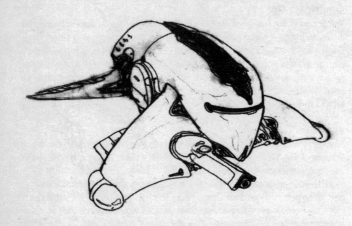

BANSHEE

Take to the skies in the Banshee, which has been improved from the original Halo. The Banshee loses height when attempting to hover, so it's best to fly it like a plane – always moving forwards. Its armour's nothing to write home about, but the fact that it's in the air makes it more difficult to hit. The Banshee has a number of defensive manoeuvres available, used by holding A and pressing different directions on the Left Analogue stick. These range from barrel rolls to loops and could prove invaluable in a dogfight. It's also possible to speed up with R, at the expense of weapons and handling. You'll find that the Banshee shows damage more readily than other vehicles, with wings and all sorts of other parts getting knocked off. Don't be fooled by this though, as you could be surprised by how long it stays airborne.

WEAPONS

Halo 2 sees the return of some old favourites, but there are plenty of new weapons in the mix, as well. Not only that, but some weapons have been re-

balanced, making them more (or less) useful than before.

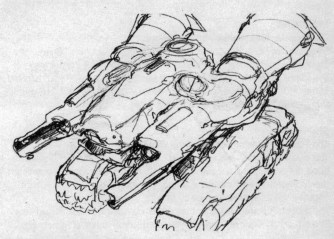

HUMAN WEAPONS

BATTLE RIFLE

Clip Size: 36   **Max Ammo:** 108   **Dual Wield:** N

The Battle Rifle fires in three-shot bursts, and is one of the most accurate weapons in the game. It's best used at medium, as its rate of fire doesn't help when enemies get in close. The Rifle has a 2x zoom, making it handy as a makeshift Sniper Rifle.

The Battle Rifle is ideal for fights when you can keep a good distance between you and your foes. Just switch to something more useful when they get close.

SMG

Clip Size: 60   **Max Ammo:** 180   **Dual Wield:** Y

The SMG's a fast-firing weapon with a large clip, but suffers from a lack of accuracy. The targeting cursor is large (meaning shots could fall anywhere inside it) and the gun recoils, moving the cursor up the screen, when fired for too long. Stick to using short, controlled bursts to combat this problem. Use the SMG at short range or against large groups of enemies. Pair it with a longer range weapon when you're outside, or you'll be sure to find yourself at quite a disadvantage.

MAGNUM
Clip Size: 12   **Max Ammo:** 48   **Dual Wield:** Y

Small clip size? Check. Not much ammo? Check. Weak shots? Check. The Pistol may have been useful in the original *Halo*, but it's not any more. The Magnum shouldn't ever be used as a primary weapon – if you're forced into it, death may not be far away. It may have decent accuracy, but you should grab something else as soon as you can.

SHOTGUN
Clip Size: 12   **Max Ammo:** 36   **Dual Wield:** N

This weapon behaves exactly as you'd expect it to. The Shotgun fires slowly, but is devastating at point-blank range. However, it soon loses its power as the distance between you and your target increases. Use this gun in tight, enclosed spaces to take enemies by surprise.

The shotgun's downside (other than the range restriction) is its reload time. This is painfully slow, but can be interrupted so you're not left defenceless.

SNIPER RIFLE
Clip Size: 4   **Max Ammo:** 20   **Dual Wield:** N

The Sniper Rifle has two levels of zoom, is incredibly accurate and is able to kill some enemies with a single shot. However, its small clip makes it terrible up close, so save it for use at long range. Ensure to carry a short-range weapon to go with the Sniper Rifle, so that you have something to fall back on if necessary.

ROCKET LAUNCHER
Clip Size: 2   **Max Ammo:** 8   **Dual Wield:** N

It's a rocket launcher – what more do you really need to know? Use it against heavily armoured vehicles, or against large groups of enemies. Just bear in mind that its clip size is extremely small and it takes quite a while to reload. Also remember to lock onto fast-moving vehicles, or distant targets, by holding R.

ENEMY WEAPONS

PLASMA PISTOL
Clip Size: n/a   **Max Ammo:** n/a   **Dual Wield:** Y

The Plasma Pistol makes a return, but is now underpowered in the same way

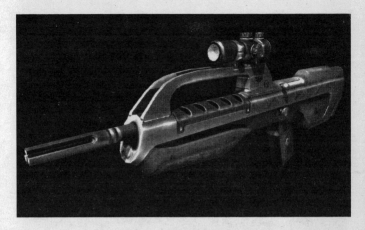

as the Magnum. It can still fire powerful, charged shots, but isn't much use against Elites – a charged shot won't break an Elite's shield and normal shots don't cause much damage. Charged shots also cause the gun to overheat, leaving you defenceless or forcing you to switch weapons. The Plasma Pistol works best when dual-wielded, but even then you might want to pick something else.

PLASMA RIFLE

Clip Size: n/a   **Max Ammo:** n/a   **Dual Wield:** Y

The Plasma Rifle remains largely unchanged in *Halo 2*. It's a fast-firing gun with good power and accuracy and will be your weapon of choice for most of the game. It's possible to dual-wield the Plasma Rifle, making it even more potent than before.

However, it is possible that the Plasma Rifle will overheat with prolonged use. Therefore, ensure to keep the trigger pressed for too long and you'll be forced to wait for it to cool down. Keep an eye on the temperature gauge or get ready to switch.

NEEDLER

Clip Size: 30   **Max Ammo:** 90   **Dual Wield:** Y

The Needler's more useful than it was before, especially when dual-wielded. Shots from this weapon home in on nearby enemies, before exploding a few

seconds later. This delay is annoying, as doomed foes still have a second or two to shoot at you before they die. Avoid using Needlers against Jackals, as shots won't get past their shields.

BEAM RIFLE
Clip Size: n/a **Max Ammo:** n/a **Dual Wield:** N

This is the Covenant's Sniper Rifle and should only be used at long range. Each shot consumes five units of battery power and it's important to keep an eye on the gun's temperature gauge. It's easy to overheat – a few shots in quick succession will do it – rendering the gun useless for a few seconds. Aim for the head (to kill enemies quicker) and then space out your shots to prevent overheating.

CARBINE
Clip Size: 18 **Max Ammo:** 72 **Dual Wield:** N

The Covenant Carbine is a powerful, single-shot rifle with a 2x zoom. The Human equivalent would be the Battle Rifle, as both are suited to fighting at medium range. However, it can be fired more times than the Battle Rifle before needing to reload. Also, as the Carbine takes ammo from a clip, there's no need to worry about overheating. Just be sure to switch to another weapon up close, as this isn't the best gun in close combat.

ENERGY SWORD

Clip Size: n/a   Max Ammo: n/a   Dual Wield: N

This is purely a close-quarters weapon. However, it shouldn't be counted out, as it is capable of killing most enemies in just a single hit. It's best to use it against powerful foes such as Brutes and Elites, as using its power on Grunts will be a waste. If you lock onto foes by waiting for the targeting cursor to turn red, you'll charge towards the enemy and let rip with an even more powerful attack.

SENTINEL BEAM

Clip Size: n/a   **Max Ammo:** n/a   **Dual Wield:** N

The Sentinel Beam is powerful and accurate, but it really eats battery power, so it won't last for long. This weapon can be put to the best use at short to medium range, as from this distance you can hold the beam steady on an opponent. As it's battery-powered, you'll also need to keep an eye on its temperature – if you hold R for too long, it'll overheat. Sentinels and Zombies seem to be weak against the Sentinel Beam, so save it for use against them.

FUEL ROD CANNON

Clip Size: 5   **Max Ammo:** 20   **Dual Wield:** N

This is the Covenant's version of the Rocket Launcher – it has a small clip, the

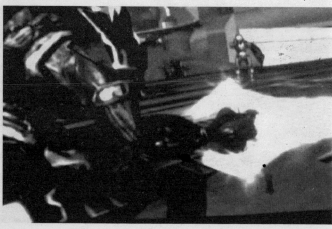

projectiles move slowly and it's slow to reload. However, it's also incredibly powerful and gives foot soldiers a chance of destroying armoured vehicles. The Cannon's also useful against Brutes and groups of enemies, as long as they're not too far away. Be careful to avoid the large green shots from these weapons when piloting vehicles of your own though, or you'll find you won't survive for long.

BRUTE SHOT
Clip Size: 4   **Max Ammo:** 12   **Dual Wield:** N
The Brute Shot is basically a grenade launcher – it fires grenades in an arc, meaning you'll need to aim slightly above your target in order to land a hit. It suffers from a small clip size, but makes up for it with sheer power. Use this at short to medium range, as it can be hard to judge the gun's arc of fire in the middle of a fight.

BRUTE PLASMA RIFLE
Clip Size: n/a   **Max Ammo:** n/a   **Dual Wield:** Y
This is an upgraded version of the Plasma Rifle and can be recognised by its distinctive red colour. It's a lot more powerful than the original, but watch out, it does overheat faster. Other than that it's identical to the one found earlier in the game.

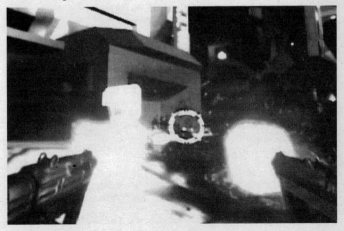

GRENADES

FRAG GRENADES
Max Ammo: 4

These are traditional grenades – throw them and, after a short delay, they go boom. They're particularly handy for throwing around corners, as they bounce off walls.

PLASMA GRENADES
Max Ammo: 4

These grenades stick to enemies, making them more useful than Frags in open combat. However, they drop straight down when they hit a wall, so they can't be thrown around corners.

DUAL WIELDING

It's possible to use two weapons at a time in *Halo 2*. Some of the larger ones are excluded from this, but most are compatible with each other.

Knowing when to dual-wield is an important aspect of the game. Doing so increases the firepower from your main weapons, but you lose the ability to throw Grenades. Here are our favourite dual-wielding combinations:

DUAL NEEDLERS
Needlers are most useful when used like this, as the rate of fire helps compensate for the delayed damage they cause.

DUAL NORMAL / BRUTE PLASMA RIFLES
Fire both Rifles at once for high damage, or alternate between them to avoid overheating and cause a steady stream of damage.

PLASMA RIFLE / SMG
Use the Plasma Rifle as the main weapon, then top it up with extra damage from the SMG when required. Just remember the SMG is slow to reload when dual-wielded.

ENEMIES

If you're going to play the single-player game before dropping into Xbox Live, you'll need to know what you're up against. Here's how to deal with the enemies in *Halo 2*:

THE COVENANT

GRUNTS

Grunts are basically cannon fodder in *Halo 2*. These cowardly creatures make up the bulk of the Covenant's forces and, for the most part, are easy to deal with. They tend to favour smaller weapons, such as Plasma Pistols and Needlers, although occasionally you'll find one with a Fuel Rod Cannon. Grunts will often run away if wounded, or if you kill too many of their friends.

The real danger with Grunts though, is that they can operate turrets. Make it a priority to kill any you see heading for one, or take out a heavy weapon and blast the turret to pieces. There's no 'ideal' weapon to use, as Grunts are vulnerable to pretty much everything – just use whatever comes to hand.

JACKALS

Jackals come in two forms – with and without shields. The shielded ones should be familiar to anyone who played the original *Halo*. Their shields deflect normal gunfire and Needler shots, but can be damaged by energy weapons. It's best to shoot Jackals from behind though, as this bypasses their shields and uses less ammo. You might also want to consider using melee attacks, as Jackals' shields won't protect them from these either.

Non-shielded Jackals usually carry Beam Rifles and attack from a distance. Your only options against these are to take part in a sniper duel, or try to sneak closer to them while making use of cover. However, neither of these methods is ideal if you're being attacked, so try to keep a wall between you and them until you've dealt with the more immediate threat.

ELITES

These enemies are reasonably powerful and come equipped with energy shields, which have to be destroyed before they can be hurt. Most weapons are capable of doing this, but it's best to steer clear of using pistols against them. Elites use a variety of weapons, ranging from Plasma Rifles to Energy Swords. Some also use camouflage similar to the type seen in the *Predator* films, while others are equipped with jetpacks. The latter are the hardest to deal with, as they move around a lot and tend to keep their distance, making them difficult to hit. Either get in close or try to lure them towards you, to make killing them easier.

HUNTERS

These are nowhere near as common as they were in the original game, which

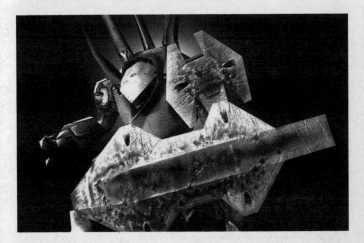

is just as well. They're still pretty nasty, as they can take an obscene amount of damage before dying. They've also got powerful beam and melee attacks, so it's best to circle around them at a safe distance to avoid getting hit.

Hunters have a weakness, though: their armour doesn't completely cover them, so shooting at the gaps helps bring them down with a minimum of fuss. The biggest gaps are found on their backs, but it's difficult to sneak up behind them unless they're focusing on another target.

DRONES

These aren't particularly strong, but they move in packs and are small and difficult to hit. They spend most of their time in the air or clinging to walls, but do land from time to time. Use automatic weapons to deal with Drones, as it's hard to hit them with single-shot guns like the Carbine or Brute Shot. Most of the time, the best you can hope for is to spray bullets in their general direction and hope that enough connect in order to bring them down.

BRUTES

Brutes are large gorilla-like creatures and are a real pain to fight. They can take plenty of damage, so you'd better have lots of ammo to hand if you want to kill them. They tend to carry Brute Plasma Rifles, Carbines and the occasional Brute Shot. However, others prefer a more old-fashioned approach and use their fists.

Make sure you've got somewhere to hide while fighting Brutes, as you'll need somewhere safe to reload – these foes absorb so much damage that you'll probably need to do so at least once during the fight. Plasma Grenades are also useful, as the Brutes' size makes them easy to hit – once a Grenade's latched on, it's bye-bye monkey!

THE FLOOD

SPORES

These are the most basic enemies in the game – their main method of attack is latching onto you and then exploding. Each Spore only causes a small amount of damage, but don't be fooled as they usually attack in vast waves and have the ability to crawl over walls and ceilings. Each one takes a single shot to kill, so it's best to use automatic weapons to fire into groups of Spores, with the SMG being ideal. The Shotgun's also a very good choice, as is the Plasma Rifle. Ensure to avoid using weapons such as the Carbine though, as doing so is a waste of ammo.

A new addition to *Halo 2* is the Spores' ability to revive fallen Zombies. Don't let them near Zombie corpses, or you might end up having to fight them all over again!

ZOMBIES

Zombies can be a real mixed bag. They take the form of most of the non-machine enemy types in the game and some are even equipped with energy shields. Zombies carry a large range of Human and Covenant weapons and can even drive vehicles. Zombies are fearsome in hand-to-hand combat, so it's best to keep out of their way whenever possible. The best way to fight them is to back away while using your chosen weapon. Sentinel Beams work well against these beasts, as do Shotguns, but only at close range. Just be careful where you step when backing away from Zombies, or you could find yourself wandering off a cliff or down a hole!

CARRIERS

The bloated-looking Carriers don't pose much of a threat. They move very slowly and can only attack by self-destructing. Shooting a Carrier will cause it to explode, damaging anything around it. The main thing about these beasts is that killing them releases a group of Spores – be prepared to fight them once the Carrier's dead, and keep them away from Zombies' corpses!

SENTINELS

Anyone who got near the end of the original *Halo* will remember these flying gun platforms. They start out weaker than they used to be, but have energy shields added to them later in the game. Sentinels can be taken out with pretty much any automatic weapon, but try to avoid using single-shot items against them, as they can be tricky to hit.

However, it's best to use the Sentinels' own weapons against them. They drop Sentinel Beams when destroyed, so grab one and give them a taste of their own medicine!

ENFORCERS

These flying monstrosities are extremely powerful and difficult to kill if you're on foot. Energy shields cover the front of Enforcers, so it's definitely best to attack from elsewhere. Enforcers fire barrages of lasers, as well as mortar rounds, both of which can kill you or destroy your vehicle before you know what's hit you.

If you're on foot, it's best to move as close to this type of enemy as you can before attacking. Try to get underneath them, where their weapons won't be able to hit you. Just remember that Enforcers will come crashing down when destroyed, so make sure you're not in the way when they land!

However, as fans will know, the real gem in the Halo 2 package is the Xbox Live multiplayer, and it's this we'll move onto next.

HALO 2 ON XBOX LIVE

Halo 2 has been a phenomenon on Xbox Live, and continues to be the dominant force in online gaming almost a year after its initial release. The game hit the shelves and greeted a public that was desperate to embrace Microsoft's new global culture, giving them a champion to lead the charge into 2005. What *Halo 2* achieved was a doubling in the Live subscription numbers in less than six months. After two years of release Live had garnered one million users, but in the period between November 2004 and May 2005, this doubled to two million because of the efforts of *Halo 2*. Sure, there were other Live enabled games available at the time, but they suffered from an unusually low user-ship because of Bungie's multiplayer beast.

As ever, *XBM* was on hand to give its verdict on the Live aspect of *Halo 2* – this part of the game scored a predictable 10/10 once again:

"Before it was even released this was tentatively labelled the finest Xbox Live shooter. Now that it's actually been out for a month, is this true? That's a rhetorical question; *Halo 2* on Xbox Live is the very definition of awesome. A reason enough on its own to get broadband installed.

However, when we first started playing the game we couldn't help but feel that Bungie had gone the way of EA. The whole lobby and game searching system is heavily geared towards clans and friends lists. You can search for game types whenever you want to, but unless you've got a group of people travelling with you in your party you'll find yourself playing against different opponents every game. Very annoying if you find a group you actually like playing with that you don't want to add to your friend list.

You do get used to this and the party system is good, but it's amazing to think that Bungie didn't think about including a classic style lobby. This takes a bit of getting used to, as does the playing style required for *Halo 2*. Kills come very swift and as a result the game can feel quite random to begin with.

It's anything but though, as both the weapon and vehicle balancing are spot on. As is the level design, which comes as a bit of a surprise following the mediocre multiplayer levels of Halo. The maps here are beautiful and, more importantly, easily remembered. You'll have your own favourite spots/routes within minutes of play. That's not to say you'll get bored of playing this, not by a long way, the sheer number of possibilities in the game modes alone will ensure that. But then you know all of this already, don't you? We can't imagine anyone out there stupid enough to not buy *Halo 2*."

However, *Halo 2* quickly started to spiral beyond that of any regular Live game. It picked up the clan aspects that had been introduced by quality Live titles such as Rainbow Six 3 Black Arrow, and applied them to its own game with devastating effect. All of a sudden, players were grouping together and challenging others to clan matches on a day-to-day basis – broadening the community aspect of Xbox Live into something approaching what Microsoft had initially dreamt the service could be. Perhaps this feeling of inclusion is one of the main reasons why the service doubled in numbers so quickly.

XBM was ready and willing to take on all comers at *Halo 2* on Xbox Live, and continues to do so with mixed success. Here are a few choice matches that the team have taken part in to date, as way of an example to illustrate how this new event gaming panned out:

MATCH 1 XBM VS SMITE THY FOE

GAME: 1
GAME: TEAM CRAZY KING
LEVEL: ASCENSION

For starters, we can say for sure that this is the purplest clan we've ever played against and, quite frankly, the whole colour co-ordination thing was a little bit intimidating. It was a fairly balanced game up until half way through when Smite Thy Foe managed to rack up a one-minute difference. We closed the gap to 15 seconds but it just wasn't enough to stop the Smite's first win.
Smite Wins

GAME: 2
GAME: ONE FLAG CTF
LEVEL: ZANZIBAR

A classic map for another classic loss by the *XBM* team. We selected a 'first to three captures' and we only managed to bag one. The game was still pretty close, though; every single round ended up as a messy yard-by-yard fight over the flag, usually with a lot of blood spilt on the seafront. During one round Smite, quite impressively, succeeded in preventing one capture within metres of the finish line.

Smite Wins

GAME: 3
GAME: TEAM SLAYER
LEVEL: COLOSSUS

As you know we're not the types to disrespect another clan, but during this round there was a lot of camping and sniping going on. After a fairly even kill-for-kill start, Smite pitched their tent in the red base with a beady-eyed sniper (Crazy Dictator, who picked up 15 medals for his accuracy) covering the approach. Despite the domination by Smite we only just lost with a final tally of 42 kills to their 50.

Smite Wins

GAME: 4
GAME: NEUTRAL BOMB
LEVEL: FOUNDATION

It's at this point we learn that two of the guys playing on the side of Smite are playing split-screen on the same telly, making clear our *Halo 2* skill… This fourth game was the longest of the lot – to call it epic would be an understatement. The game was set again as a 'first to three' and the attacks raged back and forth for a long time, each win coming down to the blink of an eye. We blinked more.

Smite Wins

GAME: 5
GAME: TEAM ROCKETBALL
LEVEL: LOCKOUT

As is becoming customary, it was down to the last game for us to save some kind of face. We decided to pick the explosive Rocketball that is always good

COLOSSUS

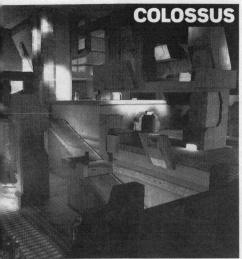

COLOSSUS

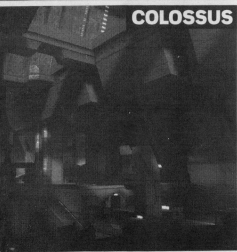

ASCENTION

ASCENTION

BURIAL MOUNDS

BURIAL MOUNDS

HEADLONG

HEADLONG

IVORY TOWER

IVORY TOWER

LOCKOUT

LOCKOUT

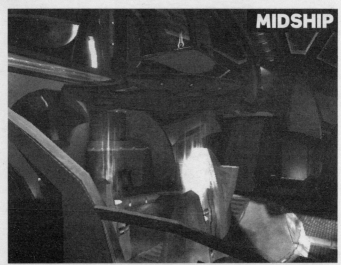

MIDSHIP

MIDSHIP

ASCENTION

ASCENTION

BURIAL MOUNDS

BURIAL MOUNDS

COAGULATION

COAGULATION

COLOSSUS

COLOSSUS

HEADLONG

HEADLONG

IVORY TOWER

IVORY TOWER

LOCKOUT

LOCKOUT

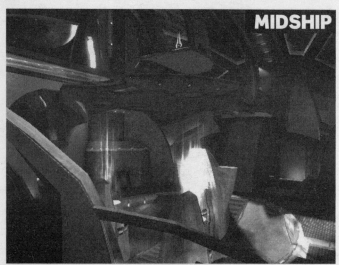

MIDSHIP

MIDSHIP

WATERWORKS

WATERWORKS

ZANZIBAR

ZANZIBAR

for a laugh, if only for the number of times the commentator shouts, "Play ball". Surprisingly, we stormed into a 30-second lead but Smite clearly weren't going to go down without a fight. Luckily, the fight wasn't enough and we salvaged a win.

XBM wins

Summary

Another loss to add to the pile for *XBM* but good fun was had by all, even if Smite Thy Foe did do a bit too much gloating after each win. Not American-style gloating you understand, just a little boast here and there, although we did catch the use of the word 'pwned' which made us die a little inside. After the match we decided to join forces and enter into a few Big Team Battle games, which reminded us how bad American gloating can be.

MATCH 2 XBM VS IPMS

GAME 1: TEAM SLAYER ON BURIAL MOUNDS

RESULT: XBM BEATS IPMS 50 TO 30

After an eternity of connection problems, lobby errors and one false start, the first game of the evening was under way. Despite attempting to distract *XBM* with their ample feminine charms (these girls are hot) the team showed little mercy during the first part of the game, racking up Double Kill and Sniper Medals with ease. Medusa and Tigerish tried to lead a PMS comeback during the final moments of the game, but it was too little too late for the girls.

XBM Wins

GAME 2: TEAM SLAYER HUMAN ON LOCKOUT

RESULT: XBM BEATS IPMS 50 TO 43

PMS chose the second map, and it was clear why. Retreating to the sniper tower, MuseChick and Medusa made short work of *XBM*'s feeble attempts to loosen their grip on the position. However, a few grenades and some heroic suicide runs from jamesTM and ZappBranniganUK, *XBM* scattered PMS, leaving AJD UK all the time in the world to pick them off from his favoured spot at the top of the warp Jump. It was a closer game, but still no cigar for the girl gamers.

XBM Wins

GAME 3: TEAM SLAYER COVENANT ON ZANZIBAR
RESULT: XBM BEATS IPMS 50 TO 42

Possibly the darkest moment of the evening for the PMS girls, this particular trip to the beach turned out to be a nightmare holiday. Tigerish dropped out half-way through the game and Harry McLegend lost no time in picking off the leaderless girls with some Covenant sniping. Medusa and Rinny made a valiant stand in the base, occasionally wiping out the entire *XBM* team in one go, but the loss of a player hit them too hard to recover. Tigerish returned, but was too late to turn the tide.

XBM Wins

GAME 4: TEAM SLAYER BLIND ON WARLOCK
RESULT: XBM BEATS IPMS 50 TO 45

Knowing they'd been beaten, the girls put on a brave face and selected Warlock as the next map. With radars off, their teamwork made short work of the *XBM* team's initial attacking, leaving PMS well up on kills. MuseChick and Rinny combined well to pick off *XBM* one by one. However, the game started to turn *XBM*'s way when the boys took up key positions on the platforms using Battle Rifles to break PMS' teamwork. We can't believe we won this one, and neither could the girls.

XBM Wins

GAME 5: TEAM SLAYER ROCKETS ON IVORY TOWER

RESULT: XBM BEATS IPMS 50 TO 28

While PMS were trying to avoid the clean sweep, *XBM* resorted to showboating in the last game, using melee attacks and the ever-popular corpsehump wherever possible. Tigerish and MuseChick made some futile attempts to hold the walkway, but AJD UK and Harry McLegend ruthlessly swept them aside, feeling only minor pangs of guilt in the process. A fifth win for the *XBM* team.

XBM Wins

Summary

Make no mistake: these girls are awesome *Halo 2* players, so our win this month surprised us as much as it did them. Perhaps *XBM* has finally found its winning player combination, or maybe the connection problems meant that the girls couldn't field their full-strength team – either way, we'll take this win and run with it. If you fancy your chances against these feisty females they'll be on tour throughout August and September. Alternatively head over to **www.pmsclan.com/uk** and check out the girls.

MATCH 3 XBM VS BUNGIE

Here at *XBM* we like to think we're pretty good at games. We play them all day. It's what we do. *Halo 2*, especially, is something we take pride in. It's played almost every lunchtime and we have a couple of genuine *Halo* machines among our ranks.

So, when the opportunity arose for some Team Slayer against the *Halo* developers themselves, the Bungie boys, we leapt at it. Sure, they made the game, they must be pretty good, but we're no slouches – we'll hold our own, probably take a couple of games off them. Hell, if our mojo is working, we could even take the duke. After all, we're *XBM*, baby.

What follows is two pages of us eating crow with a big fat helping of humble pie. Yeah, we might be *XBM*, but they're frigging Bungie, and they owned us like Amir Khan owned David Bailey. We are officially Bungie's property, and this is how it went down…

GAME 1: BACKWASH

Here's our strategy: we know the old maps pretty well, but then again, we're sure that Bungie knows them more intimately than Brad Pitt knows Angelina Jolie, so we figured that the new maps would make the playing field as even as possible.

Turns out we needn't have bothered thinking that hard.

It started well enough – AJD UK and Harry McLegend scored a couple of quick kills, and by sticking together *XBM* drew serious first blood. Then it all went pear-shaped. ZappBranniganUK lost his connection and, without our point man, we were picked off one by one. Spawning in disparate locations we were easy pickings for the well-oiled Bungie death machine – New001 had a Killing Spree, four Double Kills, one Triple Kill and a monster score of 20, equalling our entire team's output. We got served.

Time: 6:05 I Score: XBM 27, Bungie 50
BUNGIE WINS

GAME 2: ELONGATION
After a vaguely consolatory "You did well, guys" from ske7ch, we scraped our dignity off the floor and chose a map that we felt confident on, Elongation. No more hiding in the fog nonsense – time for some serious, close-quarters action. Shoot-melee-shoot, stick 'em with a grenade, wham, bam, thank you ma'am.

Sadly, the unscrupulous Bungie team must have used some illegal modding to eavesdrop, because they stole our tactics and blew us into many, tiny pieces. Harry McLegend and AJD UK pulled off a Double Kill each, but it was no match for Bungie who had six Double Kills and two Killing Sprees between them. jamesTM managed to move in for a couple of sneaky melees, but was

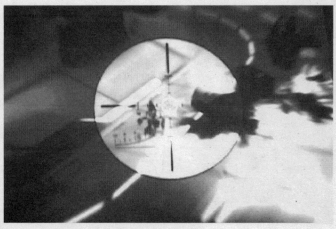

blown right through the scenery and out into space for his efforts.

Over in five minutes, and a total whitewash.

Time: 5:05 | Score: XBM 23, Bungie 50
BUNGIE WINS

GAME 3: GEMINI

Drawing a collective sigh from the team, Gemini was next. "I don't know this one, it never comes up in Matchmaking!" Like it made a difference. Having underperformed in the first two games, ZappBranniganUK and jamesTM stepped things up and led the way for XBM; jamesTM found his trusty Brute Shot for some patented cheap kills and a scorching Double Kill, and the Zapper pulled off the patented 'yOur pWN3D, l0ser!!' manoeuvre, the no-scope. That's right, WE NO-SCOPED BUNGIE! WE REALLY SHOWED THEM WHO'S BOSS! Unfortunately this didn't go down at all well and Team Bungie was merciless in its revenge, melee-ing us into bloody submission. Unable to match the awesome no-scoping, Shishka went bang-happy, sticking three of us en route to a Bungie victory in record time. Level down.

Time: 4:27 | Score: XBM 23, Bungie 50
BUNGIE WINS

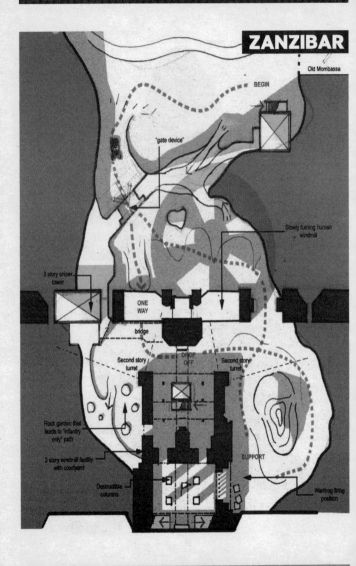

ZANZIBAR

Old Mombassa

BEGIN

"gate device"

Slowly turning human windmill

3 story sniper tower

ONE WAY

bridge

DROP OFF

Second story turret

Second story turret

AIR

Rock garden that leads to "infantry only" path

2 story windmill facility with courtyard

SUPPORT

Destructible columns

Warthog firing position

WATERWORKS

CONTROL ROOM

EARTH CITY

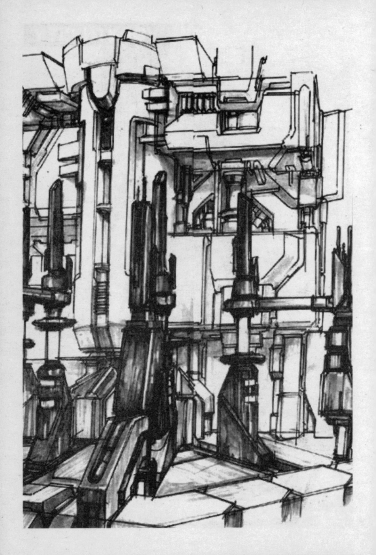

IVORY TOWER

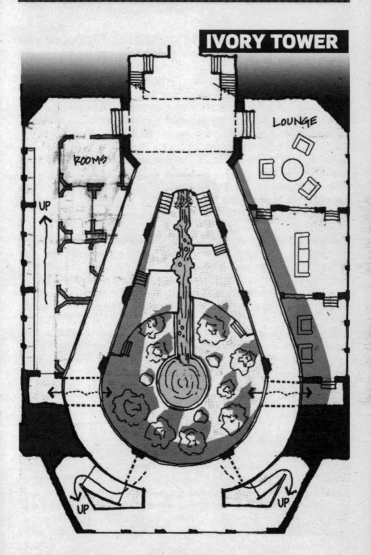

LOUNGE

ROOMS

UP

UP

UP

GAME 4: RELIC

You know how much it sucks getting sniped? How frustrating it is racing for the Sniper Rifle only to find that someone else has it, then sitting and hiding all game until you get picked off with it? Welcome to Relic, baby.

In an absolute embarrassment, Bungie proceeded to take our lunch money, give us a wedgie, put our head in the toilet and make us shine their collective shoes. Completely at their mercy, our anaemic total of 14 kills (boy, were we happy to break double figures) barely matched their Snipers Kills alone. The Zapper managed to make roadkill of a Bungie straggler, but the fun was short-lived as he also managed to reverse over jamesTM before getting blown to pieces in the Warthog.

XBM TAKES THE ROUND FROM BUNGIE! Oh wait, no we didn't.

Time: 9:51 I Score: XBM 14, Bungie 50
BUNGIE WINS

GAME 5 - TERMINAL

All hope lost, dignity long ago torn to shreds, we needed a miracle. "Get the Wraith, get the Wraith you fools!" +1 for the plan, -10 for the execution. Bungie took control of the Wraith and proceeded to decimate *XBM* in every conceivable way: sniping, splattering, big stinky Wraith cannon fire… and New001 reaffirmed his absolute dominance with two Killing Sprees and a pair of Running Riots on his way to another 20-kill total.

After arsing around trying to get the sword, jamesTM and Harry McLegend each splattered some helpless Bungie pedestrians, while ZappBrannigan and AJD UK went all GTA and jacked a couple of their vehicles… then we all ran away while they chased us in the respawned Wraith.

Clean sweep for Bungie, total rapage for *XBM*.

Time: 7:01 I Score: XBM 15, Bungie 50
BUNGIE WINS

IN MEMORANDUM

We don't really know what to say. We could go the metatextual route and argue that "We didn't lose, they won", or try the old "it's the taking part that matters" chestnut, but let's face it – we got annihilated in nothing short of Biblical fashion. Bungie were truly nice guys – they never corpsehumped, our mothers weren't mentioned and they were incredibly humble. They were a pleasure to play and very gracious winners… which actually makes things worse, because we can't take recompense from the fact that they were jerks.

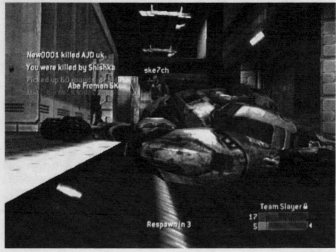

Sometimes you just gotta look in the mirror and say "Hey, we got beat – that doesn't make us any less manly." But we didn't get beat, we got boned – that makes us losers. Oh well, back to playing girls for us…"

Despite the team's shortcomings against Bungie, the mood continues to be upbeat in the *XBM* offices. So much so, that when the new multiplayer map pack came in for review, they couldn't wait to jump straight back into the *Halo 2* action. The map pack itself has sold reasonably well, but remains a specialist purchase for die-hard *Halo 2* mulitplayer fans. This is what the team thought about the new levels when they were released in July 2004:

"Why bother devoting six pages of magazine space to an expansion pack that offers little more than a handful of multiplayer maps that are of little use to anyone except devoted Live users and the odd LAN event regular? Surely everything that can be said and written about *Halo 2* has been printed, duplicated, read and forgotten by now – isn't *Halo 2* just a little bit old hat?

Well, if this really is the case, then why did the entire *XBM* team jump at the chance to spend the best part of a day trying to shoot each other to ribbons when the folks from Microsoft kindly agreed to let us loose on the new multiplayer maps ahead of general release? The simple answer is that the Multiplayer Map Pack gives a new lease of life to the finest part of the game, and this makes it an absolutely essential purchase for anyone partial to a spot of online *Halo 2* every now and again. Its Bungie's gift to the millions of faithful Live users who still relentlessly shove their Gamertags into Matchmaking for just one more session of the finest multiplayer experience on console. However, the real icing on the cake here is that this simple Map Pack will sell better than most other Xbox games, and will be played for longer than almost every other full-price title on the machine. After all, this is *Halo 2* we're talking about, and the six million Xbox owners who are in possession of a copy of the original game can't be wrong…

The question many will have been asking before the pack came on sale is whether or not it's worth the money. After all, fifteen quid for nine maps (five new ones if you already downloaded the four that became available a few months ago) seems a little steep by anyone's standards. The bonus content really isn't much to shout about, and quite frankly it's less substantial than what appears each month on our own free covermounted DVD, so this in itself is unlikely to sell the disc to the masses. Despite all this, the Multiplayer Map Pack is an absolute bargain for heavy *Halo 2* users because each new arena is so skilfully crafted and fiendishly designed that gamers really can't afford to have them missing from their collection. The level designers at Bungie have clearly set out to create the most crowd-pleasing series of stages they could, having clocked up hundreds of hours on Live watching people play and tweaking the new content accordingly. The result is a series of levels that will feel instantly familiar to old-school users of the game, without being too exclusive for relative newcomers to enjoy.

Live gamers will undoubtedly be familiar with the four existing maps – Containment, Warlock, Sanctuary and Turf – as they have been available as downloads for some time. The five new stages are Backwash – a map set in the muggy, swamp environment that made up the penultimate stage of the original Halo's single-player campaign; Relic, a mid-sized stage set around a mysterious Covenant temple founded on the Delta Halo ring; Elongation, an amusing map set on board the human space station from the start of Halo 2; Gemini, a small area set in what appears to be the religious heart of the Covenant home world; and finally Terminal, an impressive stage with origins in what seems like pre-invasion New Mombasa City. Importantly, each of the new arenas fits snugly into the overall *Halo* universe and never feel forced or out of place.

As a pack, the balance between smaller and larger maps seems to be just right, although fans of Big Team Battle or epic Team Slayer games have probably already received the majority of the better maps with Containment and Sanctuary. Relic and Terminal will probably cater for bigger parties of players, but Backwash, Elongation and Gemini are definitely more suitable for smaller Skirmishes and regular Slayer games.

One of the main differences between the new maps and the old ones is that the scenery appears so much more alive in the Map Pack stages. Aside from Zanzibar's central fan there was little in the way of scenery interaction in the original maps. The Multiplayer Map Pack now offers the chance for players to get seriously smart with the level they're playing, adding a whole new dimension to the strategic thinking behind *Halo 2*'s multiplayer. Terminal, for example, has a rail track running through the middle of the map, and every couple of seconds a high-speed train will rush through, wiping out anything on the line. This can play hell with vehicles, but at the same time can be used to shake off pursuers during a game of Capture The Flag or Assault. Similarly, Elongation has dual conveyor belts that are constantly moving large crates around the level, providing potential cover and the chance to reach better weapons with a few well-timed jumps.

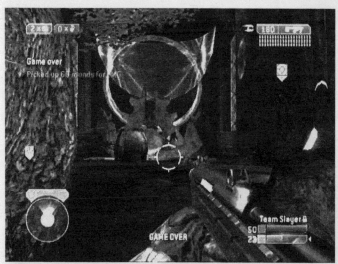

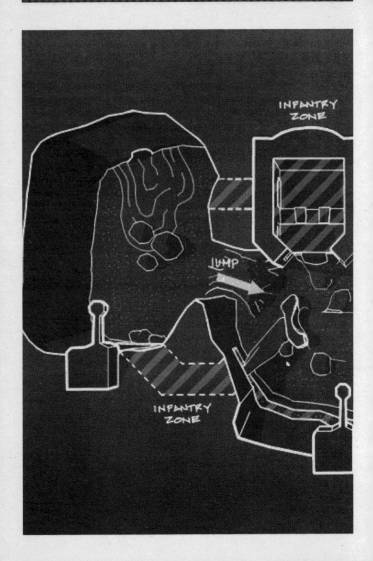

BURIAL MOUNDS

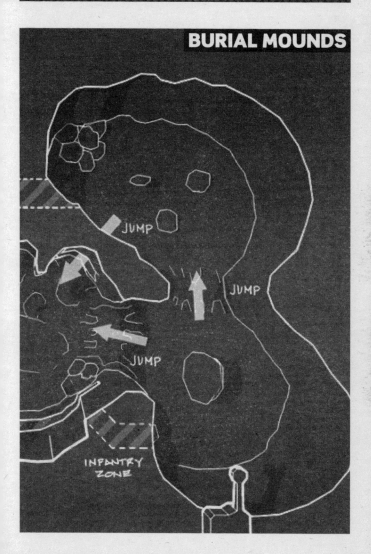

JUMP

JUMP

JUMP

INFANTRY ZONE

IVORY TOWER

LOCKOUT

Similarly, Bungie's developers seem to have been much craftier with the placement of random objects and the general layout of each level, ensuring that there are fewer and fewer opportunities for cheating and camping than ever before. Given the developer's tough stance on abuse of its prized intellectual property this comes as no surprise, but the fact that the team has been forced into thinking long and hard about how to keep the lousy cheats at bay, this has clearly had a positive effect on the design of the Map Pack levels. It would be naïve to say that the new maps are 'abuse proof' but, thankfully, there's always the possibility of a few subtle downloads every now and again to rectify the niggling problems that may arise.

If you decide to avoid paying for the new maps, don't worry – you'll still be able to play the game online as per usual. This won't change the fact that you are a contemptible buffoon, but sadly that's one thing that Bungie's coders and designers can't rectify with a Map Pack. After all, any self-respecting *Halo 2* Live player who actually misses out on these nine new maps is probably beyond help anyway..."

Anyone yet to discover the joy of *Halo 2* online will be delighted to know that the *Halo* Triple Pack is on its way this autumn. This will include *Halo*, *Halo 2*, and the Multiplayer Map Pack all for around £50. Even though all the new maps are now free, this is still a bargain for anyone yet to discover the *Halo* series (we believe there are at least two Xbox owners without a copy!)

Finally, before moving on to what lies ahead for the boys from Bungie, let's take a quick look at the basics of *Halo 2* on Xbox Live with this handy A to Z – you never know when it might come in handy…

Assault
One of the new multiplayer modes for *Halo 2* sees a fresh take on a standard concept. Players divide into teams and then battle it out to plant a bomb in the base of the opposition within a given time. The winner is either the first team to defend against or detonate the bomb. This game mode works well with the Live clan system, as it requires team-based strategy and co-operation.

Boarding
One of the new features that the world has known about for years is the ability to board. Boarding, for the uninitiated, is when the Spartan or Elite leaps onto a vehicle and kicks off its current inhabitant by use of the X button. This manoeuvre is highly risky, as being mown down by a Ghost will still result in death, but if the timing is just right it becomes an invaluable tool

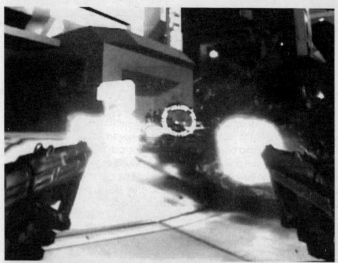

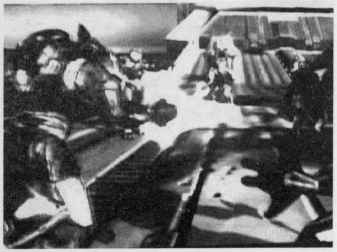

for turning defence into attack in the blink of an eye.

Clans

Clan support was always going to be an important part of Xbox Live's growth and development, so it makes sense that *Halo 2* fully supports the system that *Rainbow Six 3: Black Arrow* has championed. Use markings and emblems to make your chosen character your own and then make use of online services such as the clan-specific message boards to co-ordinate matches. Clans will be able to check out each other's stats and specific team descriptions via Live.

Dual Wielding

The much-touted dual wielding is an essential skill that has to be learned in order to survive in multiplayer. Holding the Y button over a weapon will cause your player to pick it up and use it alongside the weapon you are currently holding. Certain weapons cannot be dual wielded, such as the Shotgun and the Plasma Sword. Once in place, the second weapon will be used with the Left Trigger, and the primary with the Right as per usual.

Elite

The Covenant Elite is not only Master Chief's main rival in the single-player game, but is now a selectable character class in multiplayer. There is no obvious advantage between choosing an Elite or a Spartan, although some players will prefer to use the Covenant Carbine, Plasma rifle and Needler instead of the standard human weapons. Elites are clan customisable in the same way as Spartans, and can wield a mean Plasma Sword.

Four-player-split-screen

That's right, now four players can play online with one Live account thanks to Halo 2's split-screen options. This means that games involving sixteen players need only involve four Xbox consoles, making larger battles via Xbox Live much smoother than in other games. We would recommend an enormous TV and a top-notch sound system for this, as 12 inches split four ways on a screen with mono sound makes the game impossible to play online. You will all lose…

Guns

Much has been made of Halo 2's new weapons, but what can you expect to be dual wielding? The pistol is back in the form of the Magnum, the new Battle Rifle replaces the old Assault Rifle, the SMG is a formidable submachine gun, and of course, the shotgun makes a return along with the sniper rifle. Covenant weapons have been given an overhaul too, the Needler is much improved and the Covenant Carbine comes in a much-needed alien heavy weapon form. The Brute Shot makes its debut, and old Halo players will also be pleased to know that the Plasma Rifle and pistol are back – and they are virtually untouched.

Headlong

This map is set at the docks of New Mombasa, and as you'd expect, there is plenty of nightlife there. The map is on a fairly impressive scale, and there is plenty of earth stuff to fiddle with, hide behind, and generally break. The Battle Rifle is the key to winning this simple yet effective map.

Ivory Tower

The home of Lance O'Donnell (don't ask) this map is a bright and bloody invasion into the private life of the upper class. Festooned with fountains and marble staircases, the map is a great place for using the Plasma Sword. Watch

out for players using the lift to gain access to the upper levels of the map, as this will allow them to drop down on their unsuspecting prey.

Juggernaut

A little like the *Predator* mini-game manufactured by fans of *Rainbow Six 3: Black Arrow*, Juggernaut is a multiplayer mode that is totally new to the *Halo* series. One player starts as the Juggernaut and has all manner of weapons and abilities at their disposal with which to hunt down their opponents. Once the Juggernaut dies, the player who killed them takes over the role until they are killed and so on…

Killing (Spree)

Wipe out five or more players in a row in a multiplayer map and you'll be gifted with a killing spree award. At the end of the game the player will be awarded with a medal for this, and any other acts of heroism they managed to pull off during the game. Expect this to shoot individuals and clans up the leader boards like a rocket. Who said that violence solved nothing?

Leader

A fancy name for a host, the Leader makes the decisions during a multiplayer session, from game type to length of match, and even where the group will actually be playing their matches. It seems simple, but the leader is an important part of keeping a session together and will often be the difference between having an enjoyable online experience or an irritating one when personalities clash..

Midship

One of the multiplayer maps, Midship takes place on board a massive Covenant cruiser, the Pious Inquisitor. This vessel takes pride of place in the Covenant Navy that is assaulting the Earth, so naturally there are plenty of toys on board to play with. The level is extremely open, and is a particularly useful map for modes such as Oddball and Slayer.

No glove, no love

There are plenty of new accessories available for *Halo 2*, but we recommend keeping it simple and safe. The normal S-Pad is perfect, so avoid any custom-made gimmicks that will give you cramp in five minutes flat. In terms of headsets, why not pick up a *Halo 2* branded headset? It's comfortable, stylish, and much less cumbersome than the standard Live headset.

Oddball

Oddball is one of the new modes in Halo 2, and is a little like *Crimson Skies'* excellent Chicken download. One player or team starts with the ball and has to keep hold of it for as long as possible. The team or individual collects time by being in possession of the ball, and you guessed it, the side that hits its goals first wins the game. Easier said than done when fifteen other players are bearing down on you with Rocket launchers.

Party

We know there will be partying when *Halo 2* comes out, but the fun doesn't stop there. Party mode is where a group of players can either perform an Optimatch search or create their own game from a sort of mini-lobby. This allows groups of well-matched players, or friends, to stay together when a host quits or becomes too annoying to continue with – cutting out the need to quit, join another server, and then send out stacks of invites.

Quiet

Halo 2 multiplayer features a system that allows players to chat with anyone in the game world who is near enough to hear. This works well, as it creates a great sense of immersion into the gameplay. When strategic decisions need to be made, especially in the team-based missions, Team Talk can be achieved by holding down the talk button while barking commands.

Rockets

Rockets are an important part of Halo's multiplayer side, and they appear in a number of guises other than the standard shoulder mounted device. The new Warthog has a Rocket Launcher mounted on its rear end, and some multiplayer maps contain turrets that can be manned and fired at oncoming opponents. To add an explosive element to the Live experience, the player can select Rockets Only on some game modes.

Spartan

You can choose to play as a Spartan in *Halo 2*'s multiplayer modes. Essentially a troop along the lines of Master Chief, your main weapons will be the Battle Rifle, the Shotgun, the Pistol and the Submachine gun, although picking up Covenant devices will be an essential survival tool. Armour can be customised

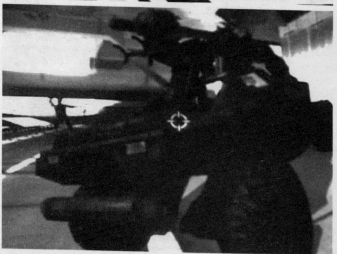

through colour, emblems and markings to make the Spartans consistent within a clan, or just to show a streak of individuality on the battlefield.

Territories

Yet another multiplayer mode, Territories allows players to battle it out in a much more cerebral way than most settings. The map has several tactical vantage points, each of which have to be captured by a team and held to collect time. Players win by collecting a set amount of time determined by the game's variants.

Ultimate Anti-son-of-a-bitch stick

The ultimate weapon in a multiplayer game of *Halo 2* has got to be the Plasma Sword. Players bemoaned the fact that they could never pick one of these up in the original, so Bungie has now heeded their demands. It's a one-shot kill weapon when charged up and locked on, but obviously this requires getting up close and personal. A great help on the more enclosed levels, but make sure you stick to long-ranged devices on the maps that take place over a grander scale.

Variants

Although *Halo 2* doesn't have a large number of multiplayer modes, it does have something fairly special under the bonnet. Each mode allows players to make alterations to the gameplay, adding twists and variations to the action. These are known as Variants and they can be added or taken away then saved as a player option file for later use. *Halo 2* will set a benchmark for online play with the choice these features bring.

Warthogs

These all-terrain darlings of the *Halo* series are available on most multiplayer maps and can be extremely useful for covering distances and gathering multiple troops in one place. Warthogs now come with either a standard chain-gun or rocket launcher attachment for mowing down enemy troops. On the down side though, Warthogs can now be boarded and destroyed, so unfortunately driving them into the thick of battle and simply flipping them back over once you've crashed may not actually be the best course of action to take anymore.

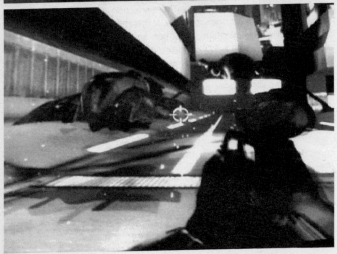

or not *Halo* would make it to
Bungie is bound for Hollywood.
industry's most powerful movie
anies want a piece of the action.
part in a joint venture that will
hired wannabes dressed up in
f the major Hollywood studios
ear the big wigs' verdicts. The
and (of *The Beach* fame) for a cool
rong start in life. However, despite
licence and a killer script, none of the
e the plunge. The reason for this is
g a hard deal – a risky proposition for
ce in the movie industry.
at the film studios would pay a ten-
t to make the movie, and they would
ver 15 per cent of the film's box office
enough, Microsoft expected the budget
ion before actor's fees are taken into
gie be given complete control over
and storyline. This tough bargaining meant
amworks, Paramount and Disney were all
withdrew from talks within 48 hours. This
sal, who were both interested but thought
a little unfair.
en the three parties reached a more suitable
Microsoft receiving $5 million for the movie
of the box office. Given the fact that over
series have been sold, this is still a substantial
t to rake in from the deal.
the revised arrangement is that Microsoft had to
control to the movie studios. How this will affect
but it's a safe bet that the Xbox manufacturer will
e as faithful to the gaming franchise as possible.
gie.net, the developer speaks in more detail about
ess came to be, and what the next steps were. As it
safely in the hands of a Universal/Fox partnership,
ed during August of this year. Alex Garland's script,

Xbox Only

Online rankings were inevitable for *Halo 2*, as almost any Xbox game with Live enabled play has this feature. Obviously the rankings denote the best players in the world at specific disciplines, and will include tables showing the most devastating clans. With millions set to buy *Halo 2*, the chances of being in the top ten are slim unless you devote a full 24 hours a day to this beauty. (*X360* accepts no responsibility for loss of social life/ malnourishment/ death as a result of this advice).

Yellow

If you're a bit of a *Halo 2* coward online, have no fear. The good people at Bungie haven't forgotten about the less-gifted Master Chiefs, and as such, they've implemented a Handicap system into the game options. This ensures that weaker players can still compete with their friends, despite their deficiencies as a *Halo 2* gamer. We understand if you need to alter this, and won't call you cheats. Honest.

Zanzibar

The *Halo 2* multiplayer map that most are familiar with, Zanzibar is a neat balance between the open levels and the more enclosed sections of *Halo 2* multiplayer. By now everyone should know that the Plasma Sword is inside the enormous spinning windmill, but other useful stuff can be found on higher vantage points such as the balcony of the human base. Human players are advised to keep the Covenant as far away from the inside of the base as possible, as once they're in, it's all over.

HALO EVOLVED >>

The speculation has been rife about whether
the big screen, but now it seems certain that
Following negotiations between some of the
studios, it seems that not one but two com
Universal and 20th Century Fox are taking
bring Master Chief to the silver screen, aft
Spartan armour, delivered scripts to each
and then waited in the various lobbies to
screenplay has been penned by Alex Gar
one million dollars, giving the project a s
the undisputable lure of such a popular
major players were initially willing to ta
because Microsoft was reportedly drivi
a PC empire with no previous experier
Microsoft's tough demands were th
million-dollar fee up front for the rig
then have to follow up by handing c
gross to the big M. As if this wasn't
to weigh in at no less than $75 mil
account, and it demanded that Bu
important aspects such as scriptin
that industry giants New Line, Dr
unable to meet demand, and th
left 20th Century Fox and Unive
the terms of the deal were still
Bargaining came to a close w
agreement – one that will see
rights, and a mere 10 per cen
11 million copies of the Halo
amount of cash for Microsof
The only real problem with
agree to cede a little of the
the film is anyone's guess,
be eager to keep the movi
In a news release on Bu
how the filmmaking proc
transpires, the film is no
the deal having been in

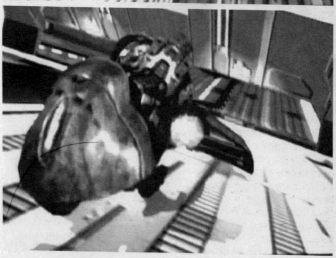

despite being doubted by some of the usual uninformed nay-sayers on the internet, has been fully approved by Bungie, and has somewhat blown the team away because of its quality and faithfulness towards the games.

The reason Garland was chosen to pen the script was because he had appeared on a list of suitable candidates supplied to Bungie by the now Producer of the *Halo* movie, Peter Schlessel. Apparently it was Garland's skill in delivering the script to *28 Days Later* that impressed the honchos at Bungie enough to hire him over the other first-rate writers that were in contention for the job. Moreover, it was his knowledge of the game that really impressed the developer, as Garland seemed to be an ardent *Halo* fan when he was approached. Speaking about his feelings towards the game, Garland commented, "My impression while playing Halo was often of being in a movie – or of having a movie come to life around me. I'm particularly thinking of moments like the fight for the beach, or the first contact Master Chief has with the Flood. So I never really thought about the 'what if' scenario, because, to my mind, something more interesting than the 'what if' was staring me in the face." This is certainly encouraging news from a fan's point of view, and when combined with the fact that Bungie has compiled an extensive

Xbox Only

Online rankings were inevitable for *Halo 2*, as almost any Xbox game with Live enabled play has this feature. Obviously the rankings denote the best players in the world at specific disciplines, and will include tables showing the most devastating clans. With millions set to buy *Halo 2*, the chances of being in the top ten are slim unless you devote a full 24 hours a day to this beauty. (*X360* accepts no responsibility for loss of social life/ malnourishment/ death as a result of this advice).

Yellow

If you're a bit of a *Halo 2* coward online, have no fear. The good people at Bungie haven't forgotten about the less-gifted Master Chiefs, and as such, they've implemented a Handicap system into the game options. This ensures that weaker players can still compete with their friends, despite their deficiencies as a *Halo 2* gamer. We understand if you need to alter this, and won't call you cheats. Honest.

Zanzibar

The *Halo 2* multiplayer map that most are familiar with, Zanzibar is a neat balance between the open levels and the more enclosed sections of *Halo 2* multiplayer. By now everyone should know that the Plasma Sword is inside the enormous spinning windmill, but other useful stuff can be found on higher vantage points such as the balcony of the human base. Human players are advised to keep the Covenant as far away from the inside of the base as possible, as once they're in, it's all over.

HALO: THE MOVIE

The speculation has been rife about whether or not *Halo* would make it to the big screen, but now it seems certain that Bungie is bound for Hollywood. Following negotiations between some of the industry's most powerful movie studios, it seems that not one but two companies want a piece of the action.

Universal and 20th Century Fox are taking part in a joint venture that will bring Master Chief to the silver screen, after hired wannabes dressed up in Spartan armour, delivered scripts to each of the major Hollywood studios and then waited in the various lobbies to hear the big wigs' verdicts. The screenplay has been penned by Alex Garland (of *The Beach* fame) for a cool one million dollars, giving the project a strong start in life. However, despite the undisputable lure of such a popular licence and a killer script, none of the major players were initially willing to take the plunge. The reason for this is because Microsoft was reportedly driving a hard deal – a risky proposition for a PC empire with no previous experience in the movie industry.

Microsoft's tough demands were that the film studios would pay a ten-million-dollar fee up front for the right to make the movie, and they would then have to follow up by handing over 15 per cent of the film's box office gross to the big M. As if this wasn't enough, Microsoft expected the budget to weigh in at no less than $75 million before actor's fees are taken into account, and it demanded that Bungie be given complete control over important aspects such as scripting and storyline. This tough bargaining meant that industry giants New Line, Dreamworks, Paramount and Disney were all unable to meet demand, and they withdrew from talks within 48 hours. This left 20th Century Fox and Universal, who were both interested but thought the terms of the deal were still a little unfair.

Bargaining came to a close when the three parties reached a more suitable agreement – one that will see Microsoft receiving $5 million for the movie rights, and a mere 10 per cent of the box office. Given the fact that over 11 million copies of the *Halo* series have been sold, this is still a substantial amount of cash for Microsoft to rake in from the deal.

The only real problem with the revised arrangement is that Microsoft had to agree to cede a little of the control to the movie studios. How this will affect the film is anyone's guess, but it's a safe bet that the Xbox manufacturer will be eager to keep the movie as faithful to the gaming franchise as possible.

In a news release on Bungie.net, the developer speaks in more detail about how the filmmaking process came to be, and what the next steps were. As it transpires, the film is now safely in the hands of a Universal/Fox partnership, the deal having been inked during August of this year. Alex Garland's script,

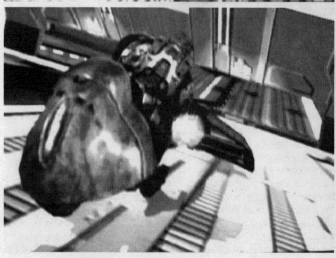

despite being doubted by some of the usual uninformed nay-sayers on the internet, has been fully approved by Bungie, and has somewhat blown the team away because of its quality and faithfulness towards the games.

The reason Garland was chosen to pen the script was because he had appeared on a list of suitable candidates supplied to Bungie by the now Producer of the *Halo* movie, Peter Schlessel. Apparently it was Garland's skill in delivering the script to *28 Days Later* that impressed the honchos at Bungie enough to hire him over the other first-rate writers that were in contention for the job. Moreover, it was his knowledge of the game that really impressed the developer, as Garland seemed to be an ardent *Halo* fan when he was approached. Speaking about his feelings towards the game, Garland commented, "My impression while playing Halo was often of being in a movie – or of having a movie come to life around me. I'm particularly thinking of moments like the fight for the beach, or the first contact Master Chief has with the Flood. So I never really thought about the 'what if' scenario, because, to my mind, something more interesting than the 'what if' was staring me in the face." This is certainly encouraging news from a fan's point of view, and when combined with the fact that Bungie has compiled an extensive

companion book that lays out absolutely every detail of the series in it – to serve as a Director's bible – all the signs are pointing towards something that is much more than the usual poor game-to-film conversion.

Garland himself is just as concerned to see his script kept as faithful to the series as possible, and he notes that, "I'd say people are right to worry. I'm worried. In fact, everyone – in particular those working on the film – should be worried. In the case of *Lord Of The Rings*, I'd guess that Peter Jackson had plenty of sleepless nights, thinking – am I doing the right thing? Am I doing the books justice? And *Lord of The Rings* shows Jackson's efforts to avoid his fears on pretty much every frame. So I'd hope the director of *Halo* has exactly the same level of commitment and concern."

The director of the film is still undecided, and Bungie is ploughing through a list of Hollywood big shots that have applied for the job. There is no word on who is actually in the running, but the chaps at Bungie.net seem extremely excited about the list of candidates that they have to choose from. Ultimately, the developer is keen to pick someone who actually knows *Halo*, and what makes the franchise tick. Let's not forget, that if the film is neglected by the fans it will make *Halo*'s future uncertain, not only as a film, but as a game too – and this is something Microsoft simply cannot allow to happen.

The film is reaching the actual creative stage at the moment, and a tentative street date has been pencilled in for 2007, by which time the world may well have seen a third game in the series. Who knows? Perhaps we'll see both the game and the film hitting the streets at exactly the same time. Stranger things have happened.

WHAT NEXT FOR HALO?

WHAT NEXT FOR HALO?

So, what is next for the *Halo* series? The official movie is in the works over in Hollywood, the novels continue to be churned out, and *Halo 2*'s Matchmaking playlists are being constantly updated. Is this enough for the millions of *Halo* fans worldwide, who are all looking to the future and the Xbox 360? Well in a word, no.

What of a next-generation instalment of *Halo*? Bungie has already announced that it is working on a new project, and chances are, it'll probably be some sort of sci-fi themed first-person shooter featuring a chap in green armour and a massive circular series of planets. Assumptions aside, there is very little that can be said about the next *Halo*, if it even exists. It has been well documented that Bill Gates wants to pit *Halo 3* against the launch of the PS3 – a bit of a no-brainer in terms of aggressive business tactics. What could be better to spoil the launch of one console than the release of its main competitor's killer app? However, this is little more than a vague promise to the legions of faithful Xbox owners who will undoubtedly be lining up a space in their living rooms for a shiny new Xbox 360. Sure, *Halo 2* will be playable on the new console, as Microsoft has promised backwards compatibility for all its top games; but next to the new breed of titles, it may start to lose its appeal very quickly. Yes, the multiplayer side of *Halo 2* is unlike anything we've seen so far, but place that next to the likes of *Perfect Dark*, *Quake 4*, *Project Gotham Racing 3* and *Ghost Recon: Advanced Warfighter*, and it could start to grow old and painfully last generation.

So what can Xbox 360 owners realistically expect to see in a next-generation version of *Halo*? Well, aside from the fact that the visuals are guaranteed to be the most beautiful sight ever witnessed on console, there are bound to be massive improvements on the gameplay and overall scale of the game. We're talking about the ability to travel an entire Halo ring seamlessly, to fight the Covenant on any part of the world, and to be able to explore every inch in your own time. Anyone who has seen the asteroid sequence from the *Prey* demo will be well aware of what the Xbox 360 is capable of in terms of sheer scale. In addition to this, there could be literally thousands of troops on the screen at one time, each with their own separate AI routine, making for truly epic battles between Marines and the Covenant.

In terms of multiplayer, 50 players will probably be a standard by the time *Halo 3* emerges, so you can certainly expect at least this many players involved in the action. A map editor seems likely as well, to add to the standard Match options that were expanded upon in *Halo 2*, and chances are, players will be given many more Live options to streamline the experience further.

In addition, expect old maps to return, along with many of the favoured weapons from the last two games.

Aside from these few general assumptions, it really is impossible to tell what might be included in the new *Halo*. The capabilities of the Xbox 360 are still unknown, even to the top developers working on key titles for the console's launch, so there can be no telling where the *Halo* odyssey will actually end. All we can do for now is buckle up, wait for more news at next year's E3 Game Show in May, and practise our shooting on Xbox Live. After all, practice makes perfect – something that the boys at Bungie would certainly be able to tell you.

THE FANS

The *Halo* fan community has been fiercely loyal to Bungie's series ever since the first glimpse at the original home computer version of the game, all those years ago. This collective of die-hard *Halo* players are always fiercely active on Bungie.net, either in or around the main forums, and have been indirectly responsible for the way the series has developed over the years. When planning updates to the Live version of *Halo 2*, Bungie will generally tend to look to the community for ideas about how the hardcore element has been playing the game.

However, it's not all forum posts and insular clan meets where the community is concerned, as *Halo*'s following has spread well beyond simple fan articles and chatter. The Live features in *Halo 2* have allowed enthusiasts the chance to create clans, but beyond this, the clans have taken the experience to a whole new level that often travels well beyond playing other clans on the game. One example of this is the Rockets on Prisoner Awards (now in its third year) where fans are given the chance to submit videos of their *Halo* or *Halo 2* experiences, showcasing a variety of activities that range from messing about with the game engine to mimicking famous music videos and film sequences.

Check out **http://rop.thatweasel.tv/** for more information on these killer movies, including details on how to download the winners and watch them for yourself. Hopefully this will inspire players to take up the gauntlet next year, and submit short films of their own.

If that is a little too hardcore for your own tastes, then why not start small and create a persona in some of the Bungie.net community forums. There are plenty to choose from and each has its own particular focus so that gamers can find specific advice when they need it. Here is a quick rundown of the major divisions:

The Underground

A general meeting place where fans can talk about anything and everything Bungie. This means that The Underground is the most likely place you'll still find discussion on Bungie's older games, such as *Myth*, *Marathon* and *Oni*. Check it out if you need to know more about the developer.

The Septagon

The Septagon is the real heart of the Bungie.net community and is where the most intense and dedicated of all fans can be tracked down. This is definitely the place to go for real specifics on the background and mythology of *Halo*.

New Mombasa

An ideal spot for anyone struggling with the single player campaign, New Mombasa is dedicated to the main story mode of *Halo 2*. Check out these forums for info on each of the levels, along with any secrets that Bungie may have left in there, like Skulls, mysterious messages, and the Scarab Gun.

Zanzibar

The place to be for anything and everything that is *Halo 2* multiplayer. This is the perfect location for smack talking about other gamers, along with a heavy mixture of tactical discussions, map glitches, and every other aspect of the game that will give you the edge over other Live gamers.

Optimatch

This one varies from Zanzibar in that it's the place for specific discussions about Matchmaking and Custom game types. If you need any ideas about how the elite are playing their private games, then log onto this site.

The Maw

The best place to visit if you're playing *Halo* on the PC or Mac. This site is probably the location you'll need to go to for advice on the more technical aspects of running *Halo* on and offline. It's also one of the last bastions for the folks who still despise the Xbox and Microsoft for buying Bungie...

THE BUNGIE STORE AND OTHER STUFF

So you've joined a clan, submitted a video, and posted all over the forums. What's next? Well, you'll probably want to kit yourself out in some of the latest Bungie merchandise – and there's plenty to choose from. Access the store from Bungie.net and you'll be presented with a wealth of swag options that range from T-shirts and caps, all the way through to little Master Chief trinkets such as note-pads, luggage tags and beer steins.

The whole range of *Halo* action figures are also available from this site, but be warned, the cost of importing anything from the US to the UK is still pretty high, so our advice is to opt for a bulk order rather than picking individual items at a time.

In September 2005, following the tragedy of Hurricane Katrina in the southern States of America, Bungie began donating all of its profits from the store to aid the relief effort in New Orleans, so there's never been a better time to buy some swag from the official Halo 2 shop.

If you don't fancy paying to import goods from Bungie.net then simply check out ebay.co.uk, as this auction site usually has everything featured on Bungie.net and more. There are always a few fan-created curiosities on the site, so it's definitely worth checking every now and again to see what has been uploaded.

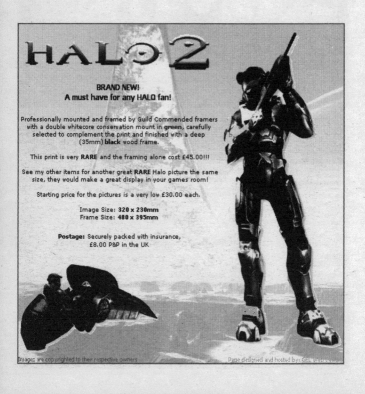

HALO 2

BRAND NEW!
A must have for any HALO fan!

Professionally mounted and framed by Guild Commended framers with a double whitecore conservation mount in **green**, carefully selected to complement the print and finished with a deep (35mm) **black** wood frame.

This print is very **RARE** and the framing alone cost £45.00!!!

See my other items for another great **RARE** Halo picture the same size, they would make a great display in your games room!

Starting price for the pictures is a very low £30.00 each.

Image Size: **320 x 230mm**
Frame Size: **480 x 395mm**

Postage: Securely packed with insurance,
£8.00 P&P in the UK

Images are copyrighted to their respective owners

The Underground

Discussions about anything and everything Bungie (view)

Forums Help

 The Septagon

Improve the Seventh Column and take over the world (view)

 New Mombasa

Dedicated forum for Halo 2 related discussions (view)

 Zanzibar

Dedicated forum for Halo 2 Multiplayer related discussions (view)

 Optimatch

Dedicated forum for Halo 2 Xbox Live Optimatch Playlist Discussions (view)

The Maw

Dedicated forum for Halo PC related discussions (view)

The Library

Dedicated forum for Halo Xbox related discussions (view)